Corn Cookery

Corn Cookery

SHEILA BUFF

LYONS & BURFORD, PUBLISHERS

 All inquiries should be addressed to: Lyons & Burford, 31 West 21 Street, New York, NY 10010.

Printed in the United States of America
Illustrations © by Leslie Watkins
Design by Wendy Palitz
10 9 8 7 6 5 4 3 2 1

Library of Congress Cataloging-in-Publication Data

Buff, Sheila.
Corn cookery / Sheila Buff.
p. cm.
Includes index.
ISBN 1-55821-245-0
1. Cookery (Corn) I. Title.
TX809.M2B84 1993
641.6'567—dc20 93-35394
CIP

Contents

Introduction

From its beginnings as a wild grass in the highlands of Mexico some seven thousand years ago, corn (or Zea mays, *to be scientifically accurate) has been a staple food for the peoples of the Americas. The triad of corn, beans, and squash was the dietary foundation for the great civilizations of the Aztecs, the Mayas, the Incas, and many native peoples of what is now the United States. And with the help of local Indians, the colonists at Plymouth Rock avoided starvation by* managing to produce a corn crop in 1621. Later settlers followed their example and planted corn. By the beginning of the nineteenth century, corn was becoming an important crop in Europe, Asia, and Africa as well. Even so, about half the world's corn is still grown in the United States. Today the annual American corn harvest consists of about eight billion bushels, worth some $20 billion. About 45 percent of this amount becomes animal feed, primarily for cattle, chicken, and hogs—which means that every time you consume milk, dairy products, eggs, or meat, you are indirectly consuming corn. Another 25 percent or so is stockpiled, and about 17 percent is exported, chiefly to Japan and Russia. Almost 6 percent is used to produce sweeteners. Of the rest, some goes for ethanol production, starch, and seed. Only about 1.4 percent ends up directly on the American table as food in the form of kernels or cornmeal. Even so, that's a lot of corn—about four bushels a person every year.

The corn we do eat arrives on the table in any one of several forms. Cornmeal is milled from dent corn, so called because the dried kernels have a dimple or dent on the top. Corn kernels are cut from sweet corn, also sometimes called green or field corn. Sweet, crunchy corn on the cob is grown from hybrid corn varieties with names such as Peaches and Cream, Early Sunglow, and Silver Queen. Popcorn is made from small, hard kernels with a relatively high moisture content.

Corn cuisine reaches its peak in the varied and subtle cooking of Mexico. Despite the importance of corn in the American *economy and diet, we remain a wheat-oriented society, eating corn mostly in a few simple, routine preparations. The astonishingly varied and subtle corn cuisine of Mexico, for example, usually reaches the American table only in the somewhat distorted form of Tex-Mex cooking. The goal of this book is to present some of the many ways corn can be used in nutritious, imaginative, and tasty dishes.*

The recipes in this volume often call for corn kernels. Ideally, the kernels should be cut from the cobs of perfectly fresh corn. To do this, husk the corn and trim off the stem end flush with the base of the ear. Hold the corn upright on its base on a cutting board. Using a small, sharp knife, slice off the corn kernels as close to the cob as you can. One plump ear of corn generally yields about half a cup of kernels. If fresh corn is not available, substitute an equal amount of drained and rinsed canned corn kernels or thawed frozen kernels. Whether you use fresh, canned, or frozen kernels, simply add them to the recipe as called for; there is no need to cook the kernels first. The recipes also often call for butter, eggs, and cream or buttermilk. To lower the fat and calorie contents of these dishes, try substituting an equal amount of vegetable or corn oil for the butter, two egg whites for each whole egg, and an equal amount of plain, low-fat or nonfat yogurt for cream or buttermilk. On the whole, corn is a flexible and forgiving food that will repay experimentation with good results.

CHAPTER
1

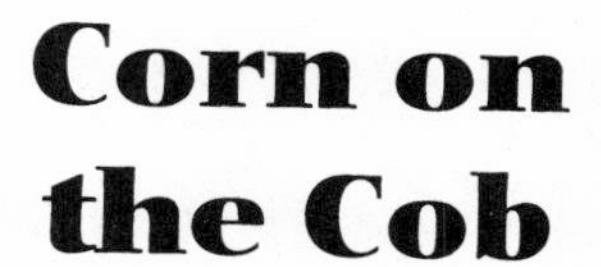

Corn on the Cob

For corn lovers, summer doesn't truly begin until early July, when the first fresh corn of the season arrives at the local farm stands. This is the taste of summer: slender ears of corn cooked briefly in boiling water, slathered with butter, sprinkled with salt and a dash of black pepper, and eaten with gusto.

Eight Ways to Cook Corn on the Cob

General Information

Always use the freshest corn possible and cook it as soon as possible. If the corn must be stored, even briefly, refrigerate it in the husk. The perfect ear of fresh corn has a bright green, flexible husk and a dark-brown, slightly sticky tassel. *Never* buy corn that has a yellowed or dry husk. The ear should be heavy and full. On the inside, the perfect ear has plump, shiny, evenly spaced kernels that spurt out a milky liquid when punctured. All corn will have some immature kernels at the tip of the ear. On perfect corn, the immature tip is small and fresh looking, not shriveled.

When husking fresh corn, you may occasionally run across a caterpillar. Don't panic. Toss the caterpillar out the door for the birds to eat and carry on. Often the ear shows no damage, or the damage is confined to the very tip. You can simply cut off the damaged part with a sharp knife and proceed as usual.

To husk corn, pull down the husk and silk from the tassel toward the stem. Break off the stem just below the base of the ear. Use your fingers to remove as much of the remaining silk as possible. It's not necessary to remove every last bit of silk, but if you really must, do it gently with a soft vegetable brush under running water.

The husks and silk can be added to the compost pile. The corncobs can also be added, but put them through a shredder first.

Method 1: In Boiling Water

Fill a pot large enough to hold all the corn two-thirds full of fresh water. Cover the pot and bring the water to a rolling boil over high heat. Add the husked corn and cook, covered, for 3 minutes (or, as the Shakers used to say, for as long as it takes to say the Lord's Prayer three times fast). Remove and serve at once.

Method 2: In Cold Water

Fill a pot large enough to hold all the corn two-thirds full of fresh, cold water. Add the husked corn and bring the water to a boil over high heat. Remove the corn when the water reaches a rolling boil and serve at once.

Method 3: In the Microwave

Note: This method is designed to cook four ears of corn at a time.

Place the husked ears in a single layer in a microwave-safe 10-inch dish. Cover the dish with microwave-safe plastic wrap, leaving a vent in one corner. Microwave on high for 2 minutes per ear, rotating the dish a quarter turn after every 2 minutes. Let stand, covered, for 5 minutes before serving.

Method 4: On the Grill in the Husk

Soak the unhusked ears in a large bucket of cold water for 2 to 3 hours before cooking. Place the ears on a hot grill (or under the broiler about 5 inches from the heat) and cook, turning often, for about 15 minutes, or until the husks are blackened on the outside. Do not overcook. Strip off the husks and silk (one person wearing heavy work gloves can do this quickly) and serve at once.

Method 5: On the Grill, Husked

Place the husked ears on a hot grill (or under the broiler about 5 inches from the heat) and cook, turning often, for about 7 minutes, or until the kernels are very hot but not browned. Do not overcook. Serve at once.

Method 6: Roasted in the Oven

Peel back the husks, remove the silk, and pull the husks up to cover the corn again. Using strips of husk or pieces of string, tie the husks closed at the tips. Soak the ears in a large bucket of cold water for 2 to 3 hours before cooking.

To cook, preheat the oven to 400°. Wrap each ear of corn tightly in aluminum foil and roast in the oven for 45 minutes. Unwrap the ears, remove the husks, and serve at once.

Method 7: When the Corn Isn't Fresh

If you must cook corn that was not picked the same day, or if you must use frozen ears (thaw them before cooking), combine 3 quarts water, 1 quart milk, and 8 tablespoons (1 stick) unsalted butter in a large pot. Bring the liquid to a boil and add the corn. Cook for 5 minutes, drain, and serve.

Method 8: Turrones

Sugared ears of corn are a popular street food in South America. This is a good way to use frozen corn (thaw it before cooking) or corn that is not perfectly fresh. It makes a somewhat offbeat dessert that is particularly popular with kids.

Preheat the oven to 400°. For each ear of corn, place 2 ounces dark brown sugar in a heavy skillet. Cook the brown sugar over moderate heat, stirring often, until it has melted into a thick syrup. Arrange the husked ears in a heavily greased baking dish. Pour the sugar syrup over the ears and cook, turning once, for 10 to 12 minutes, or until the sugar is thickened and slightly crusted.

Hot Buttered Corn

Fresh corn on the cob is delicious by itself, but butter (never margarine) makes it even better. The most commonly used technique for buttering corn—using a knife to slither a melting butter pat along a curving surface—is also very inefficient. Rolling the ear full-length on top of a stick of butter is effective but leaves the butter looking the worse for wear. Really well-organized cooks provide each diner with a little dish of melted butter and a small brush, but somehow this takes away from the essential informality of corn on the cob. An easy solution to the butter problem is to place a largish pat of butter on a piece of bread, and then use the bread to butter the corn. Of course, then eat the bread, now imbued with a delicious corn flavor.

Corn purists insist on plain, unsalted butter. Just as eating corn on the cob calls for relaxed table manners, however, the butter standard can be loosened a little as well. Try some of these flavored butters for variety.

Fresh Herb Butter

Any fresh herbs, singly or in combination, can be used to make this butter. Parsley, dill, basil, chives, and the like are all good choices.

8 tablespoons (1 stick) unsalted butter
2 teaspoons finely chopped fresh herbs

Cut the butter into small pieces and let soften to room temperature in a small bowl. Stir in the chopped herbs and blend well.

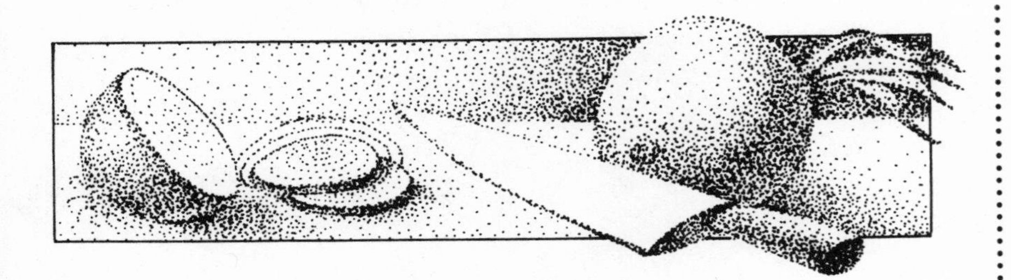

Lemon Pepper Butter

8 tablespoons (1 stick) unsalted butter
1/4 cup lemon juice
1/2 teaspoon salt
freshly ground black pepper to taste

Melt the butter in a small saucepan over low heat. Remove from heat and stir in the lemon juice, salt, and lots of black pepper. Pour the butter into a small serving dish. Let cool to room temperature and serve.

Pesto Butter

Use only fresh basil leaves to make this butter.

8 tablespoons (1 stick) unsalted butter
1/4 cup finely chopped fresh basil leaves
1 clove garlic, finely chopped
2 tablespoons grated Parmesan or Romano cheese

Cut the butter into small pieces and let soften to room temperature in a small bowl. Stir in the basil, garlic, and cheese and blend well.

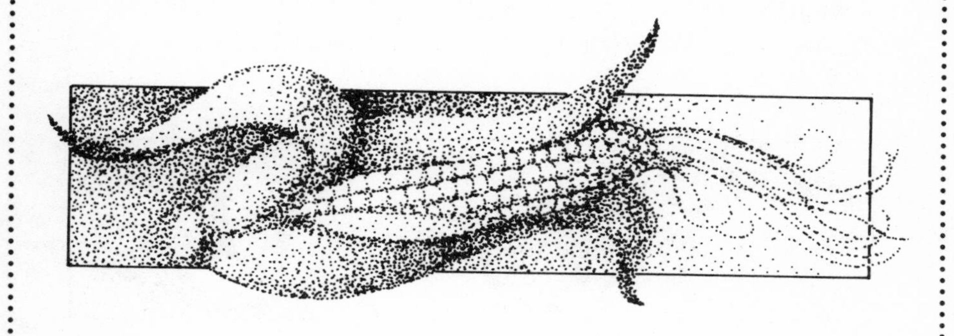

CHILI BUTTER

8 tablespoons (1 stick) unsalted butter
2 scallions, finely chopped
1 clove garlic, finely chopped
1½ tablespoons ground red chili powder
1 teaspoon lime juice

Cut the butter into small pieces and let soften to room temperature in a small bowl. Stir in the scallions, garlic, chili powder, and lime juice and blend well.

CAJUN BUTTER

8 tablespoons (1 stick) unsalted butter
1½ teaspoons paprika
1 teaspoon dried thyme
1 teaspoon dried oregano
½ teaspoon salt
¼ teaspoon cayenne pepper
freshly ground black pepper to taste

Melt the butter in a small saucepan over low heat. Remove from heat and stir in the paprika, thyme, oregano, salt, cayenne and black pepper. Pour the butter into a small serving dish. Let cool to room temperature and serve.

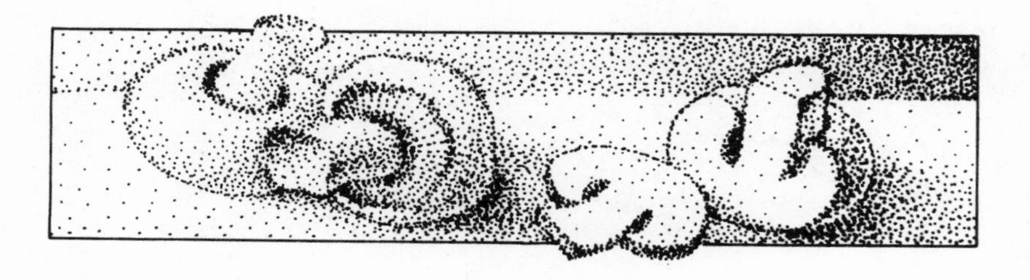

Oriental Butter

8 tablespoons (1 stick) unsalted butter
1 teaspoon soy sauce
1 teaspoon Chinese five-spice powder

Melt the butter in a small saucepan over low heat. Remove from heat and stir in the soy sauce and five-spice powder. Pour the butter into a small serving dish. Let cool to room temperature and serve.

Black Pepper Oil

An interesting change from butter. Use only the best olive oil.

4 large garlic cloves
8 tablespoons extra-virgin olive oil
1½ teaspoons coarsely ground black pepper
1 teaspoon salt

Peel the garlic cloves and crush them with the side of a heavy knife blade. Place the garlic and the olive oil in a small saucepan and cook over medium heat until the garlic just begins to brown. Turn off the heat, remove the garlic cloves, and add the black pepper and salt to the hot oil. To serve, brush the oil onto the corn with a pastry brush.

CHAPTER 2

Soups

The corn recipes in this chapter have been influenced by a wide range of cuisines: Native American, traditional American, Mexican, Italian, even Chinese. Corn lends itself particularly well to cream-based soups such as that comforting American classic, corn chowder.

Corncob Stock

Good cooks abhor waste. This elementary recipe uses corncobs to make a delicately flavored, somewhat sweet stock that is an excellent base for vegetable or cream soups. Corncob stock can be used instead of water or chicken or beef broth in soups, stews, and other dishes.

8 corncobs (reserve the kernels for another use)
5 cups water
1 teaspoon salt
1 bay leaf

In a large pot, bring the corncobs, water, salt, and bay leaf to a boil. Reduce the heat and simmer, covered, for 20 minutes. Remove the corncobs and bay leaf. If a clear stock is desired, strain the liquid through cheesecloth.

Makes about 4 cups stock

Creamy Corn Soup

2 cups corn kernels
3 1/2 cups milk
salt to taste
hot sauce to taste
4 sprigs fresh parsley
1/2 cup heavy cream
2 tablespoons unsalted butter

In a 2-quart saucepan combine the corn kernels, milk, salt, hot sauce (use just a few drops), and parsley. Bring to a boil over moderate heat. Immediately reduce the heat to low and simmer gently for 20 minutes.

Puree the soup in a food processor or blender. Return the puree to the pot and cook over low heat until the mixture thickens slightly, about 3 to 4 minutes. Add the cream and butter and cook, stirring constantly, until the butter is melted and the cream is very hot, about 3 to 4 minutes longer. Do not let the soup boil. Serve at once.

Serves 4

Corn Bisque

2 large leeks, trimmed
2 cups corn kernels
2 tablespoons unsalted butter
1 large carrot, coarsely chopped
2 celery stalks, chopped
1 medium potato, peeled and diced
1/2 teaspoon dried marjoram
1/8 teaspoon ground thyme
1 bay leaf
salt to taste
freshly ground black pepper to taste
4 cups chicken broth
1/2 cup heavy cream

Wash the leeks very well and cut them in half lengthwise. Cut each half into very thin slices.

Coarsely puree 1 cup of the corn kernels in a food processor or blender. Reserve the remaining corn.

Melt the butter in a 2-quart saucepan over moderate heat. Add the leeks and sauté until softened, about 8 to 10 minutes. Add the corn puree, carrot, celery, potato, marjoram, thyme, and bay leaf. Season to taste with salt and black pepper. Add the chicken broth and reduce the heat. Simmer, stirring occasionally, until the potato is tender, about 20 minutes.

Add the reserved corn kernels and cook until they are heated through, about 5 minutes.

Stir in the cream and cook until the cream is very hot, about 3 to 4 minutes longer. Do not let the soup boil. Serve at once.

Serves 4

Spicy Corn and Shrimp Soup

1 teaspoon vegetable oil
½ teaspoon hot red pepper flakes
12 medium shrimp, peeled and cleaned
1 tablespoon butter
2 tablespoons olive oil
1 medium onion, finely diced
2 tablespoons flour
6 cups chicken broth
2 cups corn kernels
1 small zucchini, finely diced
1 small red bell pepper, sealed and finely diced
½ teaspoon salt
frreshly ground black pepper to taste
½ cup heavy cream
½ teaspoon grated nutmeg

Heat the vegetable oil in a heavy, 3-quart saucepan over high heat. Add the hot red pepper flakes and the shrimp and sauté until the shrimp are cooked through, about 5 minutes. Remove the shrimp and set aside.

In the same saucepan, heat the butter and olive oil over medium heat. Add the onion and sauté until the onion is soft and begins to brown, about 5 to 6 minutes. Add the flour and cook, stirring constantly, for 1 minute. Add the chicken broth and the corn kernels. Cook, stirring constantly, until the mixture comes to a boil. Reduce the heat and simmer for 15 minutes. Add the zucchini and red pepper and season to taste with salt and pepper. Simmer until the vegetables are soft, about 15 minutes more.

Coarsely chop the reserved shrimp. Add the shrimp and the cream to the soup and heat until just simmering. Add the nutmeg and serve either hot or at room temperature.

Serves 6

CORN CHOWDER

Along with corn and cream, bacon and potatoes are the essential ingredients in a corn chowder. To make a Manhattan-style chowder, leave out the cream and substitute 1 cup tomato juice and 1 cup clam juice for the milk.

3 slices bacon, finely diced
1 onion, coarsely diced
1 stalk celery, coarsely diced
3 large potatoes, peeled and diced
2 cups chicken broth
1 bay leaf
½ teaspoon salt
2 cups milk
½ cup light cream
2 cups corn kernels
freshly ground black pepper to taste

In a large saucepan, sauté the bacon over medium heat until browned, about 7 minutes. Add the onion and cook until softened, about 5 minutes. Add the celery, potatoes, chicken broth, bay leaf, and salt. Reduce the heat to low and simmer until potatoes are tender, about 20 to 30 minutes.

Add the milk to the soup and cook until very hot but not boiling. Slowly stir in the light cream and corn kernels. Heat until very hot but not boiling. Season with lots of black pepper and serve at once.

Serves 4

Yellow Corn Soup

2 tablespoons unsalted butter
1 small onion, finely chopped
2 large yellow bell peppers, seeded and coarsely chopped
2 cups corn kernels
4 cups chicken broth
salt to taste
freshly ground black pepper to taste

Melt the butter in a 2-quart saucepan over moderate heat. Add the onion and cook, stirring often, until the onion is softened, about 5 minutes. Add the yellow pepper and corn and cook, stirring often, until the pepper is softened, about 5 minutes. Add the chicken broth and bring the soup to a boil. Reduce the heat to low and simmer for 25 minutes.

Coarsely puree the soup in a food processor or blender, in batches if necessary. Return the soup to the saucepan and bring to a boil again. Immediately remove the soup from the heat and season to taste with salt and black pepper.

Serves 4

Corn and Fresh Tomato Soup

Ripe, juicy tomatoes provide most of the liquid for this lovely coral-colored soup.

1 tablespoon olive oil
1 small onion, finely chopped
1 celery stalk, finely chopped
1 garlic clove, finely chopped
1/8 teaspoon cayenne pepper
4 cups corn kernels

4 large, very ripe tomatoes, seeded and coarsely chopped

½ cup water

½ teaspoon salt

Heat the oil in a 2-quart saucepan over moderate heat. Add the onion, celery, garlic, and cayenne and cook, stirring often, until the onion is softened, about 5 minutes. Add the corn kernels, tomatoes, water, and salt and bring the mixture to a boil. Immediately reduce the heat to low and simmer, covered, until the tomatoes are very soft, about 15 to 20 minutes.

Puree the soup in a food processor or blender, in batches if necessary. Return the puree to the saucepan and add a little more water if it is too thick. Reheat gently and serve very hot.

Serves 4

Succotash Soup

4 tablespoons unsalted butter

4 slices bacon, coarsely chopped

3 cups lima beans

3 cups corn kernels

1 cup light cream

3 cups water

salt to taste

freshly ground black pepper to taste

Melt the butter in a heavy, 2-quart saucepan over moderate heat. Add the bacon and cook until it is browned.

Add the lima beans, corn, cream, and water. Season to taste with salt and lots of black pepper. Reduce the heat to low and simmer, covered, until the lima beans are tender, about 6 to 8 minutes.

Serves 4

Chinese Corn Soup with Crabmeat

2 tablespoons peanut oil
4 scallions, white parts only, finely chopped
1 teaspoon finely chopped fresh ginger
1 17-ounce can cream-style corn
4 cups chicken broth
2 tablespoons dry sherry or rice wine
1 tablespoon soy sauce
1/2 pound flaked crabmeat
1 teaspoon sesame oil
1 egg, lightly beaten

Heat the oil in a 2-quart saucepan over moderate heat. Add the scallions and ginger and cook, stirring constantly, for 1 minute.

Add the cream-style corn, chicken broth, sherry, and soy sauce. Reduce the heat to low and simmer until the soup is very hot and on the verge of boiling, about 10 minutes. Add the crabmeat and sesame oil.

Pour the beaten egg into the soup in a thin, steady stream, stirring gently with a fork to form threads.

Serves 4

Zuñi Corn Soup

1 tablespoon vegetable oil
6 scallions, thinly sliced
1 pound boneless lamb, cubed
6 cups beef broth
4 cups corn kernels
2 teaspoons ground red chili powder
1/2 cup chopped cilantro

Heat the oil in a heavy, 3-quart saucepan. Add the scallions and sauté, stirring often, until softened, about 3 minutes. Add the lamb and 3 cups of the beef broth. Reduce the heat to low and simmer, stirring occasionally, until the meat is tender, about 1 hour. Skim the surface after cooking for 15 minutes.

Add the remaining beef broth, corn, and chili powder. Stir well and simmer until the corn is tender, about 15 minutes longer. Stir in the cilantro and serve.

Serves 4

Corn and Cheese Soup with Chilies

2 tablespoons unsalted butter
2 tablespoons vegetable oil
1 large onion, finely chopped
3 garlic cloves, finely chopped
2 tablespoons flour
3 cups corn kernels
2 4-ounce cans green chilies, seeded and chopped
2 large, ripe tomatoes, seeded and coarsely chopped
3 cups chicken broth
2 cups heavy cream
1½ cups shredded Muenster cheese
⅛ teaspoon cayenne pepper

Melt the butter with the oil in a 2-quart saucepan. Add the onion and garlic and sauté, stirring often, until the onion is softened, about 5 minutes. Sprinkle with the flour and cook, stirring constantly, for 2 minutes longer.

Add the corn, chilies, tomatoes, and chicken broth. Bring to a boil, then reduce the heat to low and simmer, stirring occasionally, until the corn is tender, about 15 minutes.

Add the cream and cheese to the soup. Cook, stirring often, until the cheese has melted and the cream is very hot, about 5 minutes. Do not let the soup boil. Stir in the cayenne pepper and serve at once.

Serves 4

Tortilla Soup

This simple soup is an excellent way to use up leftover tortillas.

4 tablespoons vegetable oil
8 stale corn tortillas, cut into thin strips
2 medium tomatoes, seeded and chopped
1 large onion, finely chopped
1 garlic clove, finely chopped
6 cups chicken broth
2 teaspoons ground red chilies
1 cup grated mild Cheddar or Monterey Jack cheese
1 small, ripe avocado, peeled and thinly sliced

Heat the vegetable oil in a heavy, 2-quart saucepan over moderate heat. Add the tortilla strips and fry until they are golden, only about 10 to 20 seconds. (Fry the tortillas in batches if necessary.) Drain on paper towels.

Pour off all but 1 tablespoon oil from the saucepan and add the tomatoes, onion, and garlic. Cook, stirring often, until the onion is softened, about 5 minutes. Add the broth and ground chilies and bring the soup to a boil. Reduce the heat and simmer for 10 minutes.

To serve, divide the tortilla strips evenly among individual deep soup bowls. Ladle the broth over the tortilla strips and garnish each serving with shredded cheese and avocado slices.

Serves 4

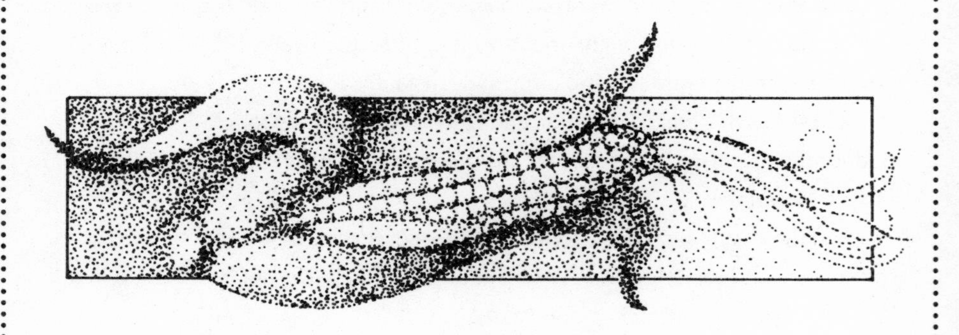

Sopa de Lima

Lime and tortilla soup is a specialty of the Yucatán region of Mexico.

4 tablespoons vegetable oil
8 stale corn tortillas, cut into thin strips
2 medium tomatoes, seeded and chopped
1 large onion, finely chopped
1 garlic clove, finely chopped
1 green bell pepper, seeded and finely chopped
6 cups chicken broth
2 cups shredded cooked chicken
2 cups corn kernels
1/3 cup finely chopped cilantro
1/2 teaspoon dried oregano
salt to taste
freshly ground black pepper to taste
3 tablespoons lime juice
1 lime, thinly sliced

Heat the vegetable oil in a heavy, 2-quart saucepan over moderate heat. Add the tortilla strips and fry until they are golden, only about 10 to 20 seconds. (Fry the tortillas in batches if necessary.) Drain on paper towels.

Pour off all but 1 tablespoon oil from the saucepan and add the tomatoes, onion, garlic, and green pepper. Cook, stirring often, until the onion is softened, about 5 minutes. Add the chicken broth, shredded chicken, corn kernels, cilantro, oregano, and salt and black pepper to taste and bring the soup to a boil. Reduce the heat and simmer for 10 minutes.

Add the lime juice and simmer for 30 seconds more.

To serve, divide the tortilla strips evenly among individual deep soup bowls. Ladle the soup over the tortilla strips and garnish each serving with lime slices.

Serves 4

Gumbo Soup

2 tablespoons olive oil
1 large onion, finely chopped
2 celery stalks, finely chopped
1 large green bell pepper, seeded and finely chopped
1 large carrot, finely chopped
1 large potato, peeled and coarsely chopped
½ teaspoon oregano
½ teaspoon ground thyme
½ teaspoon dried basil
2 bay leaves
1 14-ounce can whole tomatoes, chopped (with juice)
3 cups chicken broth
1 cup corn kernels
1 cup sliced fresh okra
1 tablespoon cider vinegar
salt to taste
freshly ground black pepper to taste
hot red pepper sauce to taste

Heat the oil in a 2-quart saucepan over moderate heat. Add the onion and sauté, stirring often, until it is softened, about 5 minutes. Add the celery, green pepper, carrot, potato, oregano, thyme, and basil. Cook, stirring often, until the vegetables are softened, about 10 minutes longer.

Add the bay leaves, tomatoes, and chicken broth. Simmer, stirring occasionally, for 10 minutes. Add the corn, okra, and vinegar and season to taste with salt, black pepper, and lots of hot red pepper sauce. Simmer until the okra is tender, about 10 to 15 minutes longer.

Serves 4

Incavolata

This hearty Italian bean soup is thickened with cornmeal.

1 tablespoon olive oil
4 garlic cloves, finely chopped
6 cups cooked cannellini beans
4 cups chicken broth
3 tablespoons tomato paste
½ teaspoon dried sage
1 teaspoon salt
freshly ground black pepper to taste
4 cups coarsely chopped fresh kale
½ cup cornmeal or masa harina
2 tablespoons lemon juice
½ cup cold water
grated Parmesan cheese

Heat the olive oil in 3-quart saucepan over moderate heat. Add the garlic and sauté, stirring often, for 1 minute. Add 3 cups of the beans and 2 cups of the chicken broth.

Puree the remaining beans and chicken broth with the tomato paste in a food processor or blender. Pour the puree back into the soup and stir well. Add the sage, salt, and lots of black pepper.

Add the chopped kale, stir well, and reduce the heat to low. Simmer until the kale is tender, about 30 to 40 minutes.

In a small bowl combine the cornmeal, lemon juice, and water. Stir well to break up any lumps. Pour the cornmeal mixture into the soup while stirring constantly. Simmer, stirring often to prevent sticking, until the soup is nicely thickened, about 10 to 15 minutes longer. Serve at once, topped with lots of Parmesan cheese.

Serves 4

Chicken and Corn Soup with Rivels

Rivels—tiny dumplings—are a specialty of the Amish. Thin egg noodles may be substituted, but the flavor is not at all the same.

1 tablespoon vegetable oil
2 celery stalks, finely chopped
1 large carrot, finely chopped
1 onion, finely chopped
6 cups chicken broth
3 cups shredded cooked chicken
3 cups corn kernels
salt to taste
freshly ground black pepper to taste

Rivels

3/4 cup flour
1/4 cup cornmeal
1/8 teaspoon salt
1 egg, beaten
1/4 cup milk or a little more

Heat the oil in a 3-quart saucepan over moderate heat. Add the celery, carrot, and onion and cook, stirring often, until the onion is softened, about 5 minutes. Add the chicken broth, shredded chicken, and corn. Season to taste with salt and black pepper. Lower the heat and simmer for 20 minutes.

While the soup simmers, prepare the rivels. In a mixing bowl combine the flour, cornmeal, salt, and egg. Add 1/4 cup milk and mix with your fingers until the mixture resembles coarse crumbs (add a bit more milk if necessary). Shape the mixture into balls the size of small marbles.

Drop the rivels into the soup and simmer until they are cooked through, about 15 minutes longer.

Serves 4

CHAPTER
3

Main Dishes

Corn is a nutritious food that is also high in fiber, very low in fat and sodium, and contains only about 140 calories per cupful. ❧ *An excellent source of complex carbohydrates, corn is also high in vitamins B and C; yellow corn also contains a goodly amount of vitamin A.* ❧ *Clearly, then, as an ingredient in a main course, corn adds lots of good nutrition.* ❧ *It also adds color, texture, and a subtle sweetness that gives depth to the dish. Corn enhances lots of dishes, but it is a particular boon to meatless meals. In vegetarian dishes, particularly those containing beans or dairy products, the incomplete amino acids in corn combine with those in the other ingredients to form complete proteins.*

Vegetarian Dishes

End-of-Summer Casserole

What to do with all those unripe tomatoes left on the vine as the first frost approaches? Use them in this hearty casserole.

1 tablespoon vegetable oil
2 cups corn kernels
3 green or red bell peppers, scaled and coarsely chopped
2 large green tomatoes, cored, seeded, and diced
3 garlic cloves, finely chopped
1 cup chopped scallions
2 teaspoons ground cumin
1 teaspoon dried oregano
2 teaspoons dried basil
1/4 cup chopped fresh parsley
freshly ground black pepper to taste
cayenne pepper to taste
1/2 cup chopped green olives
1 4-ounce can green chilies, seeded and diced
1/2 cup shredded mild Cheddar or Monterey Jack cheese
4 eggs
1/2 cup plain low-fat yogurt
paprika to taste

Preheat the oven to 375°.

Heat the oil in a large skillet over medium heat. Add the corn kernels, peppers, tomatoes, garlic, and scallions and cook until the peppers just begin to soften, about 5 minutes. Add the cumin, oregano, basil, parsley, and black pepper and cayenne to taste. Cook for 5 minutes more.

Remove the skillet from the heat and stir in the olives and chilies. Add the shredded cheese and stir until it melts. Spread the mixture evenly in a greased 9-inch baking dish.

Beat the eggs and yogurt together in a mixing bowl. Pour the egg mixture over the vegetable mixture in the baking dish and sprinkle with paprika to taste.

Bake uncovered until the casserole is nicely browned on top, about 30 to 35 minutes.

Serves 4

Portuguese Vegetable Stew

3 tablespoons olive oil
1 large onion, coarsely chopped
4 garlic cloves, finely chopped
5 potatoes, quartered
2 carrots, thickly sliced
2 tablespoons paprika
1 cup water
1 28-ounce can whole tomatoes, chopped (with juice)
2 bay leaves
1 cup dry red wine
1 cup cut green beans
3 cups sliced mushrooms
1 cup corn kernels
salt to taste
freshly ground black pepper to taste

In a large pot, heat the olive oil over moderate heat. Add the onion and garlic and cook, stirring often, until the onion softens, about 5 minutes. Add the potatoes, carrots, and paprika and cook, stirring constantly, for 3 to 4 minutes longer.

Add the water, tomatoes, bay leaves, and wine. Cover the pot, lower the heat, and simmer for 10 minutes.

Add the green beans and mushrooms and continue to simmer, covered, for 30 minutes, stirring occasionally. Add the corn kernels and simmer for 15 minutes longer, or until the potatoes are tender. Season with salt and black pepper to taste.

Serves 4

MOLE DE OLLA

This Spanish-style stew or *mole* is traditionally cooked in a large clay pot—an *olla.*

3 tablespoons olive oil
2 medium onions, coarsely chopped
2 garlic cloves, finely chopped
2 tablespoons chopped green chilies
1/2 teaspoon cinnamon
1/4 teaspoon ground cloves
4 potatoes, cut into 2-inch chunks
1 28-ounce can whole tomatoes, chopped (with juice)
2 cups cut green beans
1 small zucchini, thickly sliced
1 small yellow squash, thickly sliced
2 cups corn kernels
salt to taste
2 cups shredded mild Cheddar or Monterey Jack cheese

In a large pot, heat the olive oil over moderate heat. Add the onions, garlic, and chilies and cook, stirring often, until the onion softens, about 5 minutes. Add the cinnamon, cloves, and potatoes and cook, covered, for 5 minutes longer. Add the tomatoes and green beans and cook, covered, for 5 minutes more.

Lower the heat and add the zucchini, yellow squash, and corn kernels. Simmer, covered, until the potatoes are tender, about 25 minutes longer. Add salt to taste and serve in individual bowls topped with shredded cheese.

Serves 4

SOUTHWESTERN FRITTATA

A frittata is a hearty omelet cooked in a heavy skillet or baked in the oven. This version can be served hot, warm, or cold, making it an excellent brunch or buffet dish.

3 tablespoons olive oil
1 medium onion, chopped
1 large green bell pepper, seeded and coarsely chopped
1 large red bell pepper, seeded and coarsely chopped
2 jalapeño peppers, seeded and finely chopped
8 eggs
½ teaspoon salt
cayenne pepper to taste
5 tablespoons cornmeal
1 cup shredded mild Cheddar or Monterey Jack cheese

Preheat the oven to 350°.

In a large, heavy cast-iron skillet, heat the olive oil over moderate heat. Add the onion, red and green peppers, and jalapeño peppers and cook, stirring often, until the onion is lightly browned, about 8 to 10 minutes.

In a mixing bowl, whisk together the eggs with the salt and cayenne pepper. Whisk in the cornmeal, 1 tablespoon at a time, until it is all mixed in and there are no lumps.

Pour the egg mixture evenly over the vegetables in the skillet. Sprinkle the shredded cheese over the top. Place the skillet in the oven and bake until the eggs are set and the cheese is melted, about 12 to 15 minutes. Let the frittata stand for 5 minutes before cutting into serving wedges.

Serves 4

CORN AND CHEDDAR QUICHE

1 9-inch pie shell
3 eggs
1 cup shredded mild Cheddar cheese
1 cup corn kernels
2 scallions, finely chopped
1 4-ounce can green chilies, seeded and finely chopped
1 tablespoon minced pimento
1 cup milk
2 teaspoons ground red chili powder
½ teaspoon ground cumin
1 small avocado, peeled and coarsely chopped

Preheat the oven to 425°.

Place the pie shell on a baking sheet and bake for 5 minutes. Remove the shell and reduce the oven temperature to 350°.

In a large mixing bowl, whisk the eggs until they are frothy. Stir in the cheese, corn kernels, scallions, chilies, pimentos, milk, chili powder, and cumin.

Pour the mixture into the pie crust and sprinkle evenly with the chopped avocado. Bake until the quiche is firm and lightly browned on top, about 35 to 40 minutes. Let stand for 5 minutes before cutting into serving wedges.

Serves 4

Pasta with Corn Sauce

Serve this easy dish warm or at room temperature for a late summer supper. Use only fresh basil and parsley, and use lots of black pepper. This recipe calls for thin spaghetti, but it can be made using any sort of pasta. Try it with tortellini or small ravioli.

4 large, ripe tomatoes, seeded and coarsely chopped
2 cups corn kernels
1 cup cubed mozzarella cheese
3 garlic cloves, finely chopped
1/2 cup coarsely chopped fresh basil
1/2 cup coarsely chopped fresh parsley
1/3 cup extra-virgin olive oil
salt to taste
freshly ground black pepper to taste
1 pound thin spaghetti or spaghettini
freshly grated Parmesan cheese

In a serving bowl large enough to hold the sauce and the spaghetti, combine the tomatoes, corn kernels, mozzarella, garlic, basil, parsley, olive oil, and salt and pepper to taste. Toss well and let stand at room temperature for 1 hour.

Cook the spaghetti in a large pot of boiling water until just done. Drain well and immediately add to the sauce. Toss well and serve topped with generous amounts of Parmesan cheese.

Serves 4

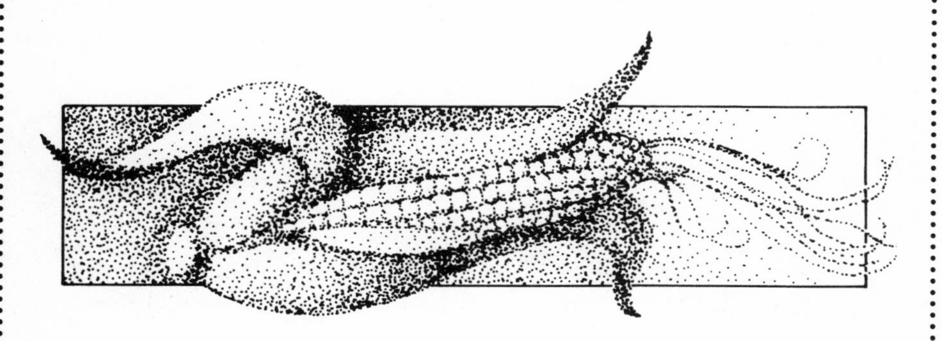

SEAFOOD

CORNMEAL CATFISH

This dish gives you the central element of a traditional fish fry. For another essential ingredient, see the recipe for hushpuppies in Chapter 10.

2 cups yellow cornmeal
1 cup flour
½ teaspoon salt
freshly ground black pepper to taste
½ teaspoon cayenne pepper
4 tablespoons ground red chili powder
2 cups buttermilk
1 egg
3 pounds catfish fillets
⅓ cup vegetable oil

Combine the cornmeal, flour, salt, black pepper, cayenne, and chili powder in a mixing bowl. Stir well.

In a shallow dish beat the buttermilk and egg together.

Dip each catfish fillet into the buttermilk mixture. Dredge each fillet in the cornmeal mixture, coating well.

In a large, heavy skillet (preferably cast-iron), heat the oil until it is very hot. (If the skillet is not large enough to hold all the fillets, use two skillets instead of cooking the fillets in two batches.) Add the catfish fillets and cook until golden on the bottom, about 3 to 4 minutes. Turn the fillets, lower the heat slightly, and cook for 1 to 2 minutes more. Drain on paper towels and serve at once.

Serves 4

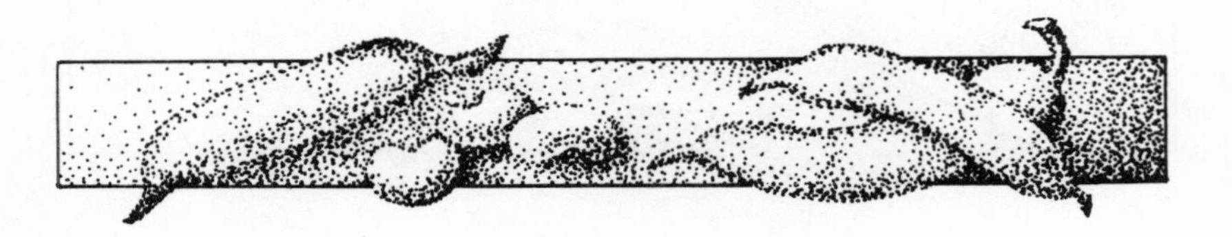

Salmon with Corn and Leeks

3 tablespoons olive oil
4 boneless salmon fillets
4 small leeks, cut lengthwise in half and thinly sliced
3 large tomatoes, seeded and chopped
4 cups corn kernels
1 tablespoon lemon juice
salt to taste
freshly ground black pepper to taste

Heat 2 tablespoons of the oil in a large, heavy skillet until very hot. Add the salmon fillets, skin-side down, and cook for 3 minutes. Turn the fillets over and cook on the other side for 3 minutes longer. Remove the fillets to a serving platter. Peel away and discard the skin.

Heat the remaining 1 tablespoon oil in the skillet over moderate heat. Add the leeks and cook, stirring often, until softened, about 5 minutes. Add the tomatoes, corn, lemon juice, and salt and pepper to taste. Cook until the tomatoes and corn are heated through, about 5 minutes longer. Divide the vegetable mixture evenly over the salmon fillets and serve.

Serves 4

Corn and Smoked Salmon Casserole

1½ cups corn kernels
2 eggs
1 cup light cream
freshly ground black pepper to taste
1 tablespoon prepared white horseradish
4 tablespoons chopped scallions
1 cup coarsely flaked smoked salmon

Preheat the oven to 350°.

Combine the corn kernels, eggs, cream, pepper, and horseradish in a mixing bowl. Whisk well to blend. Stir in the scallions and smoked salmon.

Spread the salmon mixture in a shallow, greased casserole dish. Bake until the mixture is firm and lightly browned, about 30 to 35 minutes.

Serves 4

Seafood Stew with Corn

1 pound monkfish fillets
1/2 pound scallops
1/2 cup flour
salt to taste
freshly ground black pepper to taste
1/4 teaspoon cayenne pepper
1/2 cup vegetable oil
1/2 pound shrimp, peeled and cleaned
4 tablespoons butter
3 garlic cloves, finely chopped
1 small onion, finely chopped
3/4 cup dry white wine
3/4 cup clam juice
2 cups corn kernels
2 large tomatoes, seeded and chopped
3/4 cup chopped fresh basil

Cut the monkfish fillets into 1-inch squares. If using sea scallops, cut them in half.

Combine the flour, salt, black pepper, and cayenne in a mixing bowl. Dredge the monkfish pieces and scallops in the flour.

Heat the oil in a large, heavy skillet and add the monkfish, scallops, and shrimp. (If the skillet is not large enough to hold the seafood in a single layer, cook in batches.) Cook until the monkfish and scallops just begin to brown and the shrimp begins to turn pink, about 1 to 2 minutes. Turn the seafood over and cook on the other side for 1 to 2 minutes longer. Remove the seafood from the skillet and drain on paper towels.

Pour off the oil from the skillet and add the butter. Heat the butter over moderate heat until it begins to sizzle and add the garlic and onion. Cook, stirring occasionally, for 1 minute. Add the wine and raise the heat to high. Cook, stirring constantly, until the wine is reduced by half. Add the clam juice, corn, tomatoes, and basil. Cook, stirring occasionally, for 5 minutes. Add the reserved seafood and cook until it is thoroughly hot. Serve at once in bowls.

Serves 4

Cornmeal Soft-Shell Crabs

Serve the crabs with corn salsa on the side (see Chapter 12).

2 eggs
1/2 cup yellow cornmeal
1/4 teaspoon cayenne
freshly ground black pepper to taste
8 soft-shell crabs, cleaned
2 tablespoons vegetable oil

Beat the eggs well in a mixing bowl.

In another bowl, combine the cornmeal, cayenne, and lots of black pepper.

Dip the crabs in the eggs and then dredge them well in the cornmeal mixture.

Heat the vegetable oil in a large, heavy skillet until very hot. Add the crabs and cook, turning once, until the crabs are red and the cornmeal crust is golden brown, about 5 minutes. (If the skillet is not large enough to hold all the crabs without crowding, use two skillets instead of cooking the crabs in two batches.) Serve at once.

Serves 4

Shrimp and Corn Curry

2 tablespoons vegetable oil
1 medium onion, diced
3 tablespoons mild curry powder
½ teaspoon ground cumin
1 pound medium shrimp, peeled and cleaned
2 cups cooked corn kernels
2 medium ripe tomatoes, seeded and coarsely diced
1 tablespoon finely chopped fresh ginger
1 tablespoon lemon juice
1½ teaspoons salt
freshly ground black pepper to taste
¼ cup coarsely chopped cilantro leaves

Heat the vegetable oil in a 2-quart saucepan over medium heat. Add the onion and cook until soft. Sprinkle the curry powder and cumin over the onion and cook, stirring constantly, for 1 minute.

Add the shrimp and cook, stirring often, until the shrimp are pink on all sides. Add the corn, tomatoes, ginger, lemon juice, salt, and pepper and cook, stirring occasionally, for 5 minutes longer. Serve garnished with chopped cilantro.

Serves 4

Oyster Stew with Corn

2 tablespoons butter
1 small onion, finely chopped
1 large celery stalk, finely chopped
1 small green bell pepper, seeded and finely chopped
2 garlic cloves, finely chopped
1 jalapeño pepper, seeded and finely chopped
2 scallions, finely chopped

salt to taste

1/4 teaspoon cayenne pepper

2 tablespoons flour

1 pint shelled oysters, with liquid

1 cup heavy cream

1 1/2 cups corn kernels

2 cups light cream

In a large, heavy pot, melt the butter over moderate heat. Add the onion, celery, green pepper, garlic, jalapeño pepper, scallions, salt, and cayenne and cook, stirring occasionally, until the vegetables are softened, about 5 minutes.

Sprinkle the flour over the mixture and cook, stirring often, for 3 to 4 minutes longer. Add the oyster liquid and the heavy cream and cook, stirring often, until the mixture is reduced and thickened, about 15 minutes.

Reduce the heat to low and add the corn kernels and light cream. Simmer, being careful not to let the mixture boil, for 5 minutes. Add the oysters and simmer until the oysters are cooked through, about 5 to 10 minutes longer.

Serves 4

SHRIMP AND CORN PIE

3 cups corn kernels

3 eggs, lightly beaten

3/4 cup milk or light cream

3/4 pound medium shrimp, peeled, cleaned, and cut in half

2 teaspoons Worcestershire sauce

1/4 teaspoon ground nutmeg

salt to taste

freshly ground black pepper to taste

6 tablespoons sweet butter, melted

Preheat the oven to 325°.

In a mixing bowl, combine the corn kernels, eggs, milk, shrimp, Worcestershire sauce, nutmeg, and salt and pepper to taste. Blend well.

Pour the mixture into a greased casserole dish large enough to hold it in a layer about 1½ inches deep. Dribble the melted butter over the top.

Bake until the mixture is firm and lightly browned on top, about 30 to 40 minutes.

Serves 4

Shrimp Maquechoux

Maquechoux (pronounced *mock shoe*) is a traditional Cajun dish. Why a word that literally means "mock cabbage" is applied to a spicy dish using corn kernels and cream is a mystery.

3 tablespoons unsalted butter
1 large onion, chopped
2 green bell peppers, seeded and chopped
1 red bell pepper, seeded and chopped
1 jalapeño pepper, seeded and finely chopped
1 pound medium shrimp, peeled and cleaned
4 cups corn kernels
½ cup chicken broth
½ cup chopped fresh parsley
¼ teaspoon cayenne pepper
salt to taste
freshly ground black pepper to taste
½ cup heavy cream

In a large, heavy skillet, melt the butter over medium heat. Add the onion, green pepper, red pepper, and jalapeño pepper and cook, stirring often, until softened, about 8 minutes. Add the shrimp and cook until they turn pink, about 5 minutes longer.

Raise the heat to high and add the corn, chicken broth, parsley, cayenne, and salt and black pepper to taste. Bring the liquid to a boil and reduce the heat to low. Add the heavy cream and simmer until slightly thickened, about 5 minutes. Serve immediately in deep bowls.

Serves 4

Spicy Shrimp Succotash

1½ cups cooked black beans
1½ cups cooked kidney beans
1 cup lima beans
1 cup corn kernels
1 large butternut squash, peeled, seeded, and cubed
½ cup tomato puree
1½ cups chicken broth
2 teaspoons dried marjoram
½ teaspoon salt
freshly ground black pepper to taste
½ teaspoon hot red pepper flakes
1 tablespoon vegetable oil
1 pound shrimp, peeled and cleaned
1 cup coarsely chopped cilantro leaves

In a large saucepan, combine the black beans, kidney beans, lima beans, corn kernels, squash, tomato puree, chicken broth, marjoram, salt, and lots of black pepper. Cook over moderate heat, stirring occasionally, until the squash is tender, about 20 minutes.

When the squash is just ready, heat the red pepper flakes and vegetable oil in a large, heavy skillet over high heat until very hot. Add the shrimp and cook, stirring often, until they are cooked through and pink, about 5 minutes.

Add the shrimp to the stew. Stir in the cilantro and serve at once.

Serves 4

Chicken and Turkey

Cornmeal Fried Chicken

½ cup sour cream
¼ teaspoon cayenne pepper
1 frying chicken, cut into serving pieces
¼ cup yellow cornmeal
¼ cup flour
¼ teaspoon ground nutmeg
¼ teaspoon paprika
salt to taste
freshly ground black pepper to taste
2 tablespoons bacon drippings or vegetable oil
4 tablespoons unsalted butter

In a large mixing bowl, combine the sour cream and cayenne pepper. Add the chicken pieces and turn well to coat. Let stand for 20 minutes.

In a large bowl, combine the cornmeal, flour, nutmeg, paprika, and salt and black pepper to taste. Dredge the chicken pieces in the cornmeal mixture.

In a large, heavy skillet, heat the bacon drippings and 2 tablespoons of the butter over medium heat. Add the chicken pieces and cook until golden brown all over, about 10 minutes per side. (If the skillet is not big enough to hold all the pieces, cook in batches, keeping the cooked pieces warm in the oven.) Add the remaining butter to the skillet as needed.

Serves 4

South American Chicken Stew

4 skinless, boneless chicken breast halves
2 tablespoons yellow cornmeal
1/4 cup milk
2 eggs
salt to taste
freshly ground black pepper taste
5 tablespoons vegetable oil
2 onions, coarsely chopped
4 garlic cloves, finely chopped
6 tomatoes, seeded and coarsely chopped
1/2 teaspoon hot red pepper flakes
1/3 cup chopped fresh cilantro
1 teaspoon dried oregano
1 cup chicken broth

Cut each chicken breast half into thirds.

In a large mixing bowl, combine the cornmeal, milk, eggs, and salt and black pepper to taste. Beat well.

Dip the chicken pieces into the batter and coat well.

In a large, heavy skillet, heat 2 tablespoons of the oil over moderate heat. Add the chicken pieces and cook until they are browned on all sides, about 10 minutes. Drain the chicken on paper towels.

Add the remaining oil to the skillet. Add the onions and cook, stirring often, until the onions are soft, about 5 minutes. Add the garlic, tomatoes, hot red pepper flakes, cilantro, oregano, and the cooked chicken pieces.

Add the chicken broth and bring it to a boil. Reduce the heat to low, cover, and simmer until the chicken is completely cooked through, about 10 minutes longer.

Serves 4

Chicken Maquechoux

2 tablespoons unsalted butter
1 medium onion, chopped
3 large, ripe tomatoes, peeled, seeded, and chopped
2 cups corn kernels
1 cup heavy cream
¼ teaspoon dried thyme
¼ teaspoon dried basil
2 teaspoons dried parsley
3 cups cubed cooked chicken
3 tablespoons tomato paste
several dashes hot sauce
⅛ teaspoon cayenne pepper
salt to taste
freshly ground black pepper to taste

In a large skillet, melt the butter over medium heat. Add the onion and cook, stirring occasionally, until the onion is softened, about 5 minutes. Add the tomatoes, corn kernels, cream, thyme, basil, and parsley. Lower the heat, cover, and simmer for 15 minutes. Uncover and simmer until the sauce is thickened, about 5 to 10 minutes more.

Add the chicken, tomato paste, hot sauce, cayenne pepper, and salt and black pepper to taste. Continue to cook, stirring often, until the chicken is heated through, about 10 minutes longer.

Serves 4

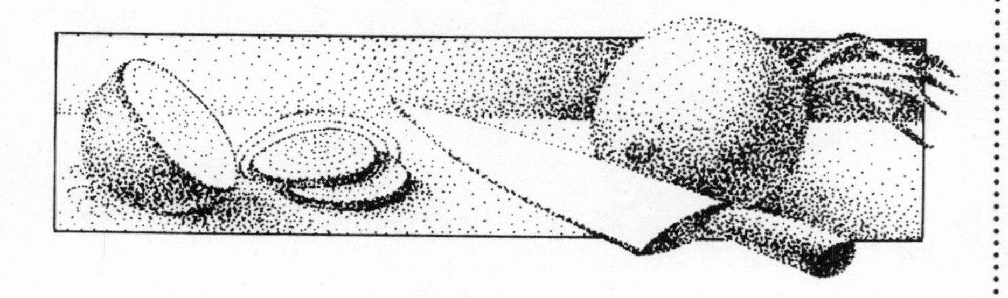

Chicken with Corn and Peppers

2 whole boneless, skinless chicken breasts
4 tablespoons vegetable oil
2 large onions, chopped
1 large green bell pepper, seeded and coarsely chopped
1 large red bell pepper, seeded and coarsely chopped
3 large, ripe tomatoes, seeded and coarsely chopped
1/2 cup chicken broth
1/4 cup chopped fresh basil
1/4 cup chopped fresh parsley
1/8 teaspoon dried thyme
1/4 teaspoon cayenne pepper
salt to taste
freshly ground black pepper to taste
3 cups corn kernels

Cut each chicken breast in half. Cut each half into pieces about 1 inch square.

In a large, heavy skillet, heat the oil over high heat. When it is very hot, add the chicken pieces and cook until they are golden on all sides, about 8 to 10 minutes. Remove the chicken to a platter and set aside.

Drain off most of the fat from the skillet and add the onions and green and red peppers. Cook over moderate heat, stirring often, until the peppers are softened, about 10 minutes. Add the tomatoes, chicken broth, basil, parsley, and thyme. Reduce the heat to low and simmer, stirring occasionally, for 5 to 7 minutes longer.

Return the chicken pieces and any juices to the skillet. Add the cayenne pepper and salt and black pepper to taste. Cook, stirring occasionally, until the chicken pieces are thoroughly cooked through, about 10 to 15 minutes. Add the corn kernels and cook until they are heated through, about 5 minutes longer.

Serves 4

Creamy Corn and Chicken Casserole

1 3–4 pound chicken, cut into serving pieces
2 tablespoons vegetable oil
3 cups corn kernels
salt to taste
freshly ground black pepper to taste
1 cup heavy cream
8 bacon slices, cut in half

Preheat the oven to 325°.

In a large, heavy skillet, heat the vegetable oil over high heat until very hot. Add the chicken pieces and cook on all sides until the chicken is golden all over, about 15 minutes.

Arrange the chicken pieces in a casserole dish large enough to hold them all in one layer. Place the corn kernels in an even layer over the chicken pieces and season with salt and pepper to taste. Pour any juices from the skillet over the corn. Pour the cream evenly over the corn. Arrange the bacon pieces evenly over the corn.

Cover the dish and bake for 30 minutes. Remove the cover and bake until the bacon is curled and crispy, about 30 to 40 minutes longer.

Serves 4

Chicken Corn Pie

This unusual dish is from South America. The recipe calls for chicken, but this is also a good use for leftover turkey.

1/3 cup dark raisins
3 tablespoons vegetable oil
2 onions, coarsely chopped
3 large tomatoes, seeded and coarsely chopped
1/2 teaspoon cinnamon
2 hard-boiled eggs, chopped

3 garlic cloves, finely chopped
3 poblano chilies, seeded and chopped
salt to taste
freshly ground black pepper to taste
4 cups cubed cooked chicken, cubed
1/4 cup chopped fresh parsley

Pie Crust

4 cups corn kernels
4 tablespoons unsalted butter
1/3 cup chopped fresh cilantro
2 teaspoons sugar
4 eggs
salt to taste
paprika for dusting

To make the filling, soak the raisins in enough warm water to cover for 5 minutes. Drain and set aside.

In a skillet heat the oil over moderate heat. Add the onion and cook until softened, about 5 minutes. Add the raisins, tomatoes, cinnamon, hard-boiled eggs, garlic, chilies, and salt and black pepper to taste. Cook, stirring constantly, for 2 to 3 minutes. Add the chicken pieces and parsley, stir well, and remove from the heat.

To make the pie crust, puree the corn kernels in a food processor or blender.

Melt the butter in a large skillet over moderate heat. Reduce the heat to very low, add the pureed corn, and stir gently. Stir in the cilantro and sugar and cook for 2 to 3 minutes. Add the eggs one at a time, mixing well after each addition. Add salt to taste. Cook, stirring constantly, until the mixture thickens. Remove from heat and let cool to room temperature.

Preheat the oven to 350°.

Grease a 2-quart casserole dish. Using about two-thirds of the corn mixture, line the bottom and sides of the dish. Fill the dish with the chicken mixture. Top with the remaining corn mixture and dust with paprika. Bake until the topping is set and browned, about 1 hour.

Serves 4

Tortilla Casserole

The growing popularity of Tex-Mex cooking means that fresh corn tortillas are easily found in the refrigerator case of your supermarket. Use up stale corn tortillas and leftover chicken (or turkey or pork) in this easy dish.

1 tablespoon vegetable oil
1 onion, chopped
3 garlic cloves, finely chopped
1 4-ounce can green chilies, seeded and chopped
2 large tomatoes, seeded and coarsely chopped
1 cup cooked black, kidney, or pinto beans
2 cups shredded cooked chicken
2 teaspoons ground red chili powder
¼ cup coarsely chopped fresh cilantro
12 stale corn tortillas, torn into bite-sized pieces
2 cups shredded mild Cheddar or Monterey Jack cheese

Preheat the oven to 375°.

Heat the vegetable oil in a large skillet over moderate heat. Add the onion and garlic and cook, stirring often, until the onion is softened, about 5 minutes. Add green chilies, tomatoes, beans, chicken, chili powder, and cilantro. Cook, stirring often, until the beans and chicken are heated through, about 5 to 7 minutes. Add the torn tortillas to the skillet and toss well.

Pour the tortilla mixture into a greased 2-quart baking dish. Bake for 30 minutes. Sprinkle with the cheese and bake until the cheese is melted, about 5 to 7 minutes longer.

Serves 4

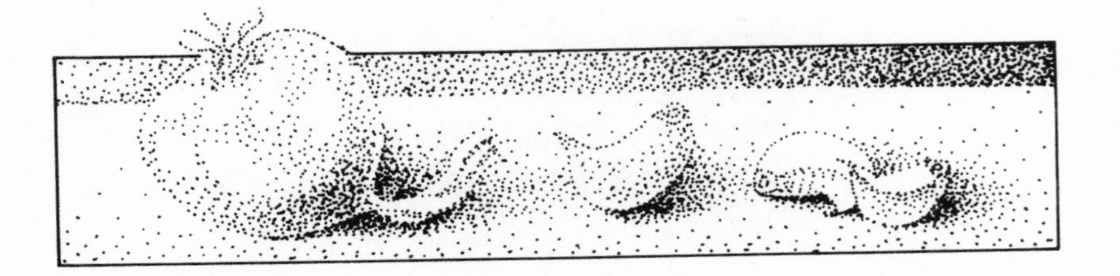

Enchilada Casserole

Enchiladas are tortillas rolled around a filling and baked.

2 tablespoons vegetable oil
1 onion, chopped
2 garlic cloves, finely chopped
2 jalapeño peppers, seeded and chopped
2 4-ounce cans green chilies, seeded and chopped
2 tomatoes, seeded and chopped
1 teaspoon ground cumin
¼ cup coarsely chopped fresh cilantro
2 cups shredded cooked chicken
10 corn tortillas
1 cup shredded mild Cheddar or Monterey Jack cheese
2 cups shredded iceberg lettuce
1 cup sour cream

Preheat the oven to 350°.

Heat the oil in a skillet over moderate heat. Add the onion and garlic and cook, stirring often, until the onion is softened, about 5 minutes. Add the jalapeño peppers, green chilies, tomatoes, cumin, and cilantro. Cook, stirring occasionally, until the tomatoes are softened, about 5 minutes. Add the chicken and cook until it is thoroughly heated, about 3 minutes longer. Set the filling mixture aside.

Heat the tortillas, one at a time, in another ungreased skillet over moderate heat. Cook for just a few seconds on each side until the tortilla is flexible. Fill each tortilla by placing a few spoonfuls of the filling at one edge. Roll the tortillas up tightly and place them, seam-side down, in a greased baking dish. Sprinkle the cheese evenly over the enchiladas and bake until the cheese is melted, about 10 minutes. To serve, sprinkle each enchilada with a portion of the shredded lettuce and top with a dollop of sour cream.

Serves 4

Turkey Cutlets with Corn and Basil

Use only fresh basil for this quick, simple, yet elegant dish.

1 1/2 pounds thinly sliced turkey cutlets
1/4 cup flour
salt to taste
freshly ground black pepper to taste
2 tablespoons olive oil
2 shallots, finely chopped
2 tablespoons red wine vinegar
2 large tomatoes, seeded and chopped
1 1/2 cups corn kernels
1/3 cup chicken broth or white wine
4 tablespoons heavy cream
1 teaspoon Dijon mustard
1/3 cup coarsely chopped fresh basil

Dredge the turkey cutlets well in the flour, shaking off any excess. Season to taste with salt and pepper.

In a heavy skillet large enough to hold the turkey cutlets in one layer, heat the oil. When it is very hot, add the turkey cutlets and cook until they are nicely browned on both sides. Remove the cutlets to a serving platter and keep warm while cooking the sauce.

Add the shallots to the skillet and cook, stirring often, until they are softened but not browned, about 3 to 4 minutes. Add the vinegar and cook, stirring often, for 1 minute. Add the tomatoes, corn, chicken broth, and any juices from the reserved turkey cutlets. Cook over high heat, stirring often, for 2 to 3 minutes longer.

Add the heavy cream and mustard to the skillet and stir until just blended. Season to taste with salt and black pepper and cook until very hot but not boiling. Stir in the basil leaves and remove from the heat. Pour the sauce over the turkey cutlets and serve at once.

Serves 4

BEEF, LAMB, AND PORK

GREENS WITH HAM AND CORNMEAL DUMPLINGS

2 tablespoons unsalted butter
1 large onion, chopped
½ pound cooked ham, cubed
1 pound Swiss chard or collard greens, trimmed and coarsely chopped
½ cup chicken broth
½ pound watercress, trimmed and coarsely chopped
½ pound arugula, trimmed and coarsely chopped
⅓ cup milk
1 tablespoon lemon juice
1 teaspoon hot sauce

Cornmeal Dumplings
½ cup flour
½ cup cornmeal
1½ teaspoons baking powder
½ teaspoon salt
1 egg

Melt the butter in a large, heavy skillet over medium heat. Add the onion and cook, stirring occasionally, until the onion just begins to soften, about 2 minutes. Add the ham and cook, stirring occasionally, for 5 minutes. Add the Swiss chard or collard greens and chicken broth, cover, and cook until the greens are wilted, about 10 minutes. Add the watercress and arugula, cover, and cook 10 minutes longer.

To make the dumplings, combine the flour, cornmeal, baking powder, and salt in a mixing bowl. Beat in the egg and milk until the mixture is smooth.

Add the lemon juice and hot sauce to the greens and stir well. Drop the dumpling batter by tablespoonfuls over the greens mixture. Cover and cook *without lifting* the lid until the dumplings are firm, about 18 minutes longer.

Serves 4

Southwestern Corncake

For authenticity, this dish calls for ingredients that are easily found in the Spanish/Mexican sections of large supermarkets: chorizos (hot Spanish sausages), green chili salsa, poblano chili peppers, and masa harina (finely ground hominy with the texture of cornmeal).

1 pound Spanish sausages (chorizos), coarsely chopped
2 eggs
1 onion, finely chopped
3 tablespoons unsalted butter, softened
1 cup sour cream
1 cup green chili salsa
1 poblano chili, seeded and chopped
1 1/4 cups masa harina
1/2 cup flour
1 teaspoon baking powder
1 teaspoon baking soda
1/2 teaspoon salt
1 cup milk
2 cups corn kernels
1 cup grated mild Cheddar or Monterey Jack cheese

Preheat the oven to 350°.

In a large, heavy skillet over medium heat, cook the chorizos until they are lightly browned. Using a slotted spoon, remove the chorizos to a dish and set aside.

Pour off all but 1 tablespoon of the fat from the skillet. Add the onion and cook until it is lightly browned, about 5 minutes. Set aside.

In a large mixing bowl, beat the eggs with the butter until well mixed. Beat in the sour cream, salsa, poblano chili, and reserved onion. Add the masa harina, flour, baking powder, baking soda, and salt. Stir well. Add the milk and stir well again. Add the corn kernels, cheese, and reserved chorizos. Stir well.

Pour the mixture into a greased 9-inch baking dish. Bake until nicely golden, about 45 minutes. Let stand 5 minutes before serving.

Serves 4

Mexican Pot Roast

Use bottom round, rump, or chuck for this dish.

2 tablespoons vegetable oil
4-pound beef roast
1 large onion, coarsely chopped
2 garlic cloves, finely chopped
1 green bell pepper, seeded and coarsely chopped
1 cup beef broth
3 tablespoons ground red chili powder
½ teaspoon cayenne pepper
½ teaspoon cinnamon
1 28-ounce can whole tomatoes, chopped (with juice)
1 teaspoon salt
3 cups cooked kidney beans
2 cups corn kernels
1 large red bell pepper, seeded and coarsely chopped
¼ cup chopped cilantro

Preheat the oven to 375°.

Heat the oil in a 6-quart flameproof casserole or Dutch oven. Add the roast and brown on all sides. Remove the roast and set aside.

Pour off all but 2 tablespoons of fat from the casserole. Add the onion, garlic, and green pepper and cook, stirring often, until softened, about 5 minutes. Add the beef broth and cook, stirring often, until the liquid comes to a boil. Reduce the heat to low.

Return the roast to the casserole. Add the chili powder, cayenne pepper, cinnamon, tomatoes, and salt. Cover the casserole and bake for 2½ hours, turning the roast every 30 minutes.

Add the kidney beans, cover, and bake for 15 minutes.

Add the corn and red pepper, cover, and bake for 15 minutes longer, or until the roast is tender.

To serve, place the roast in the center of a serving platter, surrounded by the vegetables. Sprinkle the vegetables with the cilantro.

Serves 6

STEWS

Hopi Corn Stew with Blue Dumplings

The Hopi have traditionally cultivated a hardy strain of blue corn. Blue cornmeal can be found in gourmet shops and health-food stores.

2 tablespoons vegetable oil
1½ pounds lean ground beef
1 medium onion, chopped
1 large green bell pepper, seeded and chopped
1 tablespoon ground red chili
4 cups corn kernels
1 medium zucchini, thickly sliced
1 small butternut squash, peeled, seeded, and cut into 1-inch chunks
4 to 5 cups water
2 tablespoons flour

Blue Dumplings
1 cup blue cornmeal
2 teaspoons baking powder
1 teaspoon salt
1 tablespoon bacon drippings
⅓ cup milk

In a large, heavy pot or Dutch oven, heat the oil over moderate heat. Add the chopped meat and cook until lightly browned. Add the onion, green pepper, and chili. Cook, stirring often, until the onion is softened, about 5 minutes. Stir in the corn, zucchini, and squash. Add enough water to cover and bring to a boil. Reduce the heat to low and simmer until the vegetables are tender, about 30 to 40 minutes.

In a small bowl combine 2 tablespoons of the cooking liquid and the flour. Stir well and then whisk back into the stew. Simmer until thickened, about 5 minutes longer.

To make the blue dumplings, combine the cornmeal, baking powder, and salt in a mixing bowl. Work in the bacon drippings with your fingers. Add the milk and work into the mixture. During the last 15 minutes of cooking time (but before it is time to thicken the stew), drop the mixture by tablespoonfuls into the stew. Cover the pot and *do not lift the lid* until the 15 minutes have passed.

Serves 4

CARBONADA

This is hearty Creole-style stew from Argentina.

3 tablespoons vegetable oil
2 pounds lean beef, cubed
1 onion, chopped
1 green bell pepper, seeded and chopped
2 jalapeño peppers, seeded and chopped
4 garlic cloves, finely chopped
2 tomatoes, seeded and chopped
1 bay leaf
1 teaspoon dried parsley
1 teaspoon dried oregano
½ teaspoon dried thyme
salt to taste
freshly ground black pepper to taste
1 medium sweet potato, peeled and cubed
1 medium white potato, peeled and cubed
1 cup cooked white beans
4 to 5 cups beef broth
2 tart apples, peeled, cored, and diced
2 medium zucchini, thickly sliced
1 cup corn kernels
12 dried apricots

Heat the oil in a heavy pot or Dutch oven over medium heat. Add the beef cubes and brown all over. Add the onion, green pepper, jalapeño pepper, garlic, and tomatoes. Cook, stirring occasionally, until the onion is softened, about 5 minutes. Add the bay leaf, parsley, oregano, thyme, and salt and black pepper to taste. Stir well.

Add the sweet potato, white potato, and beans. Add 4 cups beef broth, cover, and reduce the heat. Simmer until the beef and potatoes are tender, about 30 to 40 minutes. Add additional beef broth if needed.

Add the apples, zucchini, corn, and apricots. Stir well, cover, and cook until everything is thoroughly heated, about 5 minutes longer.

Serves 4

BRUNSWICK STEW

There's a town called Brunswick in Georgia. Both Virginia and North Carolina have Brunswick counties. Which is the ancestral home of Brunswick stew? Contemplate the enigma while you prepare this filling dish.

1 5-pound chicken, quartered, with giblets
3 large onions, finely chopped
3 celery stalks, finely chopped
3 large carrots, finely chopped
3 bay leaves
5 parsley sprigs
½ teaspoon dried thyme
10 whole black peppercorns
2 garlic cloves, crushed
½ teaspoon dried red pepper flakes
1 teaspoon salt
½ pound bacon, coarsely chopped
2 large tomatoes, seeded and peeled
2 tablespoons tomato paste
2 cups corn kernels

2 large potatoes, peeled and cubed
2 cups lima beans
2 cups sliced okra
1 teaspoon salt
freshly ground black pepper to taste
hot sauce to taste

Place the chicken and giblets in a large stockpot and add just enough water to cover. Add half the chopped onion, celery, and carrots, reserving the rest. Add the bay leaves, parsley, thyme, peppercorns, garlic, and red pepper flakes, cover, and simmer over low heat until the meat is very tender, about 2 hours.

Let the chicken cool in the broth. When the meat is cool enough to handle, remove it from the bones and cut the meat into small pieces. Discard the skin, bones, and giblets.

Strain the cooking liquid, discarding the solids and returning the stock to the pot. Add enough additional water to make approximately 8 cups.

In a large, heavy skillet over medium heat, cook the bacon pieces until they are crisp. Drain on paper towels and set aside. Pour off all but 1 tablespoon of drippings from the skillet and add the remaining onions, celery, and carrots. Cook, stirring often, over medium heat until the vegetables are softened, about 5 minutes. Add the tomatoes and tomato paste. Stir well and add the mixture to the stockpot.

Add the reserved chicken pieces, bacon, corn, potatoes, lima beans, and okra to the pot. Season to taste with salt, black pepper, and hot sauce. Cook over low heat, stirring occasionally, until the potatoes and other vegetables are tender, about 30 to 40 minutes.

Serves 12

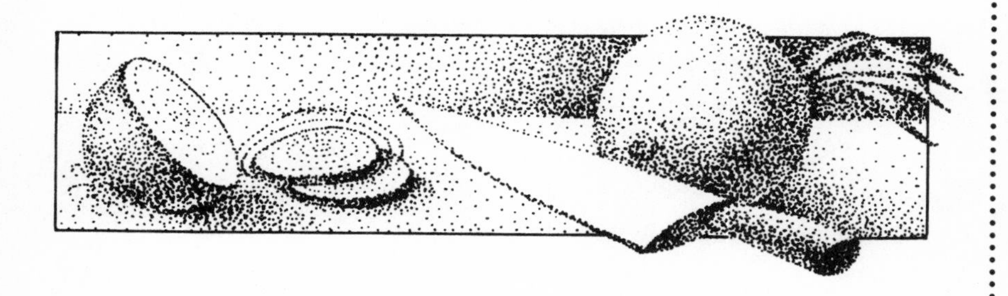

BURGOO

Both Brunswick stew and burgoo are meant to feed a crowd. The chief difference between them is that burgoo is made with lamb. Both dishes benefit from being made a day ahead.

3 tablespoons vegetable oil
3 pounds boneless lamb, cubed
1 5-pound chicken, quartered, with giblets
1 teaspoon dried red pepper flakes
1 teaspoon salt
freshly ground black pepper to taste
3 large potatoes, peeled and diced
2 large onions, coarsely chopped
3 carrots, coarsely chopped
2 cups lima beans
3 cups corn kernels
2 cups sliced okra
1 28-ounce can whole tomatoes
2 garlic cloves, finely chopped

In large, heavy skillet, heat the oil. Cook the lamb cubes until they are lightly browned all over. Remove from the skillet and set aside.

Place the chicken and giblets in a large stockpot and add the lamb cubes. Add the red pepper flakes, salt, and black pepper to taste. Add just enough water to cover and simmer, covered, until the chicken and lamb are very tender, about 2 hours. Skim occasionally.

Remove the chicken and giblets from the pot. When the chicken is cool enough to handle, remove the meat from the bones and cut it into small pieces. Discard the skin, bones, and giblets. Return the meat to the pot.

Add the potatoes, onions, carrots, lima beans, corn kernels, okra, tomatoes, and garlic to the pot. Cook over low heat, stirring occasionally, until the stew is thick and the vegetables are very tender, about 1½ hours.

Serves 12

Corn Boil

More fun than a clambake and a lot simpler. To contract or expand the recipe, use these per-person estimates: ½ pound shrimp, ¼ pound sausage, 1½ ears corn. For each gallon of water, use 2 tablespoons shrimp boil.

3 tablespoons commercial shrimp boil
1½ gallons water
2 pounds hot smoked sausage links, cut into 2-inch pieces
12 ears fresh corn, husked
4 pounds shrimp, in the shell

In a large pot, bring the shrimp boil and water to a rolling boil over high heat. Add the sausage and cook for 5 minutes. Add the corn and cook 5 minutes longer. Add the shrimp and cook 3 minutes longer. Do not overcook.

Drain immediately and serve at once, preferably on paper plates at an outdoor picnic table covered with newspaper and accompanied by lemonade and ice-cold beer.

Serves 8

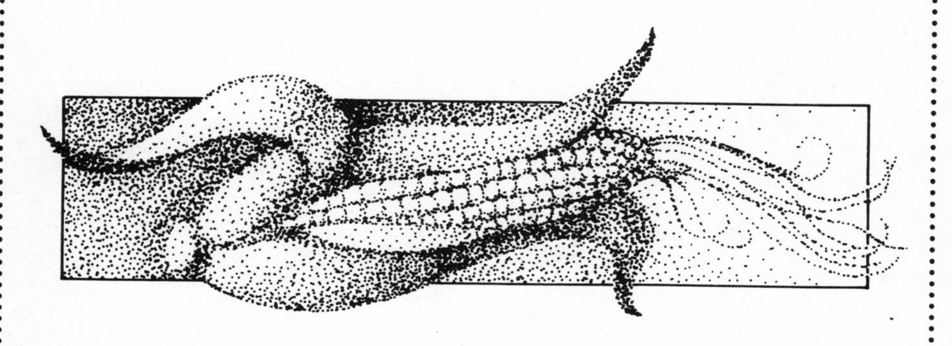

CHAPTER
4

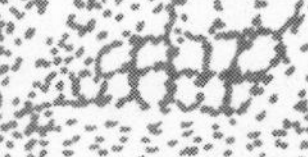

Side Dishes

Corn on the cob is not always an appropriate side dish, but there are lots of other great corn dishes that are—and that offer a welcome change from the usual potatoes, rice, noodles, and green vegetables.

Fried Corn

Remarkably, there are people who do not like to eat corn on the cob. This dish is the next best thing. If you wish, sauté a few thinly sliced scallions with the corn. You can also try adding some chopped fresh herbs, such as dill or basil, along with—or instead of—the salt and pepper.

8 ears fresh corn, husked
4 tablespoons unsalted butter
salt to taste
freshly ground black pepper to taste

Using a sharp knife, cut the kernels from the ears. With the back of the knife, scrape the ears to remove the additional milk and corn bits from the cob. There should be about 4 cups of corn.

Melt the butter in a skillet over moderate heat. Add the corn and cook, stirring occasionally so the mixture doesn't stick, until the corn is thoroughly heated, about 4 minutes. Remove from the heat, season with salt and black pepper to taste, and serve at once.

Serves 4

Creamed Corn

This rich dish is a far cry from canned cream-style corn. The canned version is thickened with cornstarch.

8 ears fresh corn, husked
4 tablespoons unsalted butter
1 cup heavy cream
salt to taste
freshly ground black pepper to taste

Using a sharp knife, cut the kernels from the ears. With the back of the knife, scrape the ears to remove the additional milk and corn bits from the cob. There should be about 4 cups of corn.

Melt the butter in a skillet over moderate heat. Add the corn and cook, stirring occasionally so the mixture doesn't stick, until the corn is thoroughly heated, about 4 minutes.

Stir in the cream and cook, stirring occasionally, until the mixture is slightly thickened, about 10 minutes longer. Remove from the heat, season with salt and black pepper to taste, and serve at once.

Serves 4

Corn with Sour Cream

8 ears fresh corn, husked
4 tablespoons unsalted butter
3 scallions, thinly sliced
1/2 cup sour cream
dash cayenne pepper
salt to taste
freshly ground black pepper to taste

Using a sharp knife, cut the kernels from the ears. With the back of the knife, scrape the ears to remove the additional milk and corn bits from the cob. There should be about 4 cups of corn.

Melt the butter in a skillet over moderate heat. Add the scallions and cook until they are softened, about 1 minute. Add the corn and cook, stirring occasionally so the mixture doesn't stick, until the corn is thoroughly heated, about 4 minutes.

Stir in the sour cream and cayenne pepper. Cook until the sour cream is just hot through, about 1 to 2 minutes; do not let the mixture boil. Remove from the heat, season with salt and black pepper to taste, and serve at once.

Serves 4

BAKED CORN

8 ears fresh corn, husked

1 tablespoon sugar

2 tablespoons flour

salt to taste

freshly ground black pepper to taste

6 tablespoons unsalted butter

Preheat the oven to 375°.

Using a sharp knife, cut the kernels from the ears. With the back of the knife, scrape the ears to remove the additional milk and corn bits from the cob. There should be about 4 cups of corn.

Combine the corn, sugar, flour, and salt and black pepper to taste in a mixing bowl.

Spread the mixture evenly in a greased 9-inch baking dish. Dot the top with the butter and bake until the top is golden brown and very crisp, about 45 minutes.

Serves 4

SOUTHWESTERN BAKED CORN

2 tablespoons vegetable oil

1 large onion, coarsely chopped

2 jalapeño peppers, seeded and finely chopped

1 14-ounce can whole tomatoes, chopped (with juice)

2 tablespoons ground red chili powder

3 cups corn kernels

1 cup grated mild Cheddar or Monterey Jack cheese

Preheat the oven to 350°.

Heat the vegetable oil in a skillet and add the onion. Cook, stirring often, until the onion is golden, about 5 minutes. Add the jalapeño peppers, tomatoes, chili powder, and corn kernels. Stir well.

Pour the mixture into a greased 2-quart baking dish. Bake for 45 minutes. Sprinkle the top with the grated cheese and continue baking until the cheese is melted and lightly browned, about 10 minutes longer.

Serves 4

Yellow Velvet

The Shakers invented this delicately flavored combination.

4 tablespoons unsalted butter
2 pounds yellow summer squash, trimmed and finely diced
2 cups corn kernels
⅓ cup heavy cream
salt to taste
freshly ground black pepper to taste

Melt the butter in a skillet over medium heat. Add the squash and cook, stirring frequently, until it is softened, about 5 minutes. Add the corn kernels and cook for 1 minute more.

Add the cream and cook, stirring constantly, until it is heated through, about 3 minutes longer. Season to taste with salt and pepper and serve at once.

Serves 4

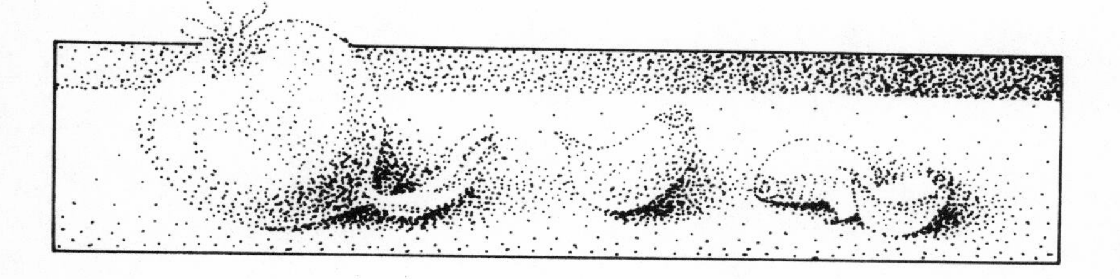

Corn and Zucchini au Gratin

Another good way to use up an end-of-summer superabundance of zucchini.

1½ pounds zucchini
3 tablespoons unsalted butter
3 tablespoons flour
1¾ cups milk
⅓ cup heavy cream
⅛ teaspoon nutmeg
⅛ teaspoon cayenne pepper
salt to taste
freshly ground black pepper to taste
¼ cup grated mild Cheddar cheese
4 cups corn kernels
¼ cup grated Parmesan cheese

Preheat the oven to 350°.

Cut the zucchini in half lengthwise. Cut each half into ½-inch slices. Steam the zucchini until it is cooked through but still firm, about 5 minutes.

Melt 2 tablespoons of the butter in a skillet over moderate heat. Whisk in the flour, stirring until it is blended. Add all the milk and whisk rapidly until the mixture is thickened and smooth. Whisk in the cream, nutmeg, cayenne pepper, and salt and black pepper to taste. Cook, stirring occasionally, for 5 minutes longer. Stir in the Cheddar cheese and remove from the heat.

Add the zucchini and corn kernels to the cream sauce. Pour the mixture into a greased 9-inch baking dish. Dot the top with the remaining butter and sprinkle with the Parmesan cheese. Bake until golden brown and bubbly, about 25 to 30 minutes.

Serves 4

Confetti Corn

1 tablespoon unsalted butter
2 tablespoons olive oil
2 green bell peppers, seeded and julienned
1 red bell pepper, seeded and julienned
1 yellow bell pepper, seeded and julienned
3 garlic cloves, finely chopped
2 cups corn kernels
6 scallions, finely chopped
salt to taste
freshly ground black pepper to taste

Melt the butter with olive oil in a skillet over medium heat. Add the julienned peppers and the garlic and cook, stirring constantly, until the peppers are softened, about 5 minutes. Add the corn and scallions and season to taste with salt and black pepper. Cook, stirring often, until the scallions are softened and the corn kernels are thoroughly heated, about 5 minutes longer.

Serves 4

Curried Corn with Peppers

1 tablespoon butter
1/3 cup chopped scallions
1 teaspoon finely chopped garlic
1 jalapeño pepper, seeded and finely diced
1 teaspoon mild curry powder
1 red bell pepper, seeded and coarsely diced
1 green bell pepper, seeded and coarsely diced
2 cups corn kernels

½ teaspoon salt

freshly ground black pepper to taste

2 tablespoons chopped coriander

Melt the butter in a skillet over medium heat. Add the scallions, garlic, jalapeño pepper, and curry powder. Cook, stirring constantly, until the scallions are soft, about 3 minutes.

Add the red and green peppers, corn, salt, and black pepper. Stir well, cover, and cook until the peppers are softened, about 2 minutes. Add the coriander, stir well, and serve.

Serves 4

Corn, Bacon, and Tomato Sauté

6 slices bacon

2 cups corn kernels

2 large cloves garlic, finely chopped

2 large, ripe tomatoes, seeded and coarsely chopped

salt to taste

freshly ground black pepper to taste

Cook the bacon until crisp in a large skillet over medium heat. Remove and drain on paper towels. Pour off all but 3 tablespoons of bacon grease.

Add the corn to the skillet and cook, stirring often, until it is just heated through, about 2 minutes.

Add the garlic and cook, stirring often, for 1 minute. Add the tomatoes and toss gently to mix. Cook, stirring gently, until tomatoes are heated through, about 2 minutes longer. Season with salt and pepper.

Crumble the bacon on top and serve at once.

Serves 4

Corn, Okra, and Tomatoes

This is a classic Southern vegetable combination, one that even confirmed okra haters have been known to eat. For true Southern flavor, use bacon grease and add the sugar.

2 tablespoons bacon grease or unsalted butter
1 large onion, finely chopped
1 large green bell pepper, seeded and coarsely chopped
3 large, ripe tomatoes, seeded and coarsely chopped
2 cups fresh okra, sliced into 1/4-inch rings
3 garlic cloves, finely chopped
2 cups corn kernels
1 teaspoon sugar (optional)
1/2 teaspoon salt
1/4 teaspoon cayenne pepper
freshly ground black pepper to taste

Heat the bacon grease in a large skillet over moderate heat. Add the onion and green pepper and cook, stirring often, until softened, about 5 minutes. Add the tomatoes, okra, and garlic. Reduce the heat to low and simmer, covered, until the okra is tender, about 15 minutes.

Add the corn kernels, sugar (if used), salt, cayenne pepper, and black pepper to taste. Cook, stirring often, for 5 minutes longer.

Serves 4

Corn with Green Beans and Mushrooms

1 pound fresh green (string) beans, trimmed
2 tablespoons unsalted butter
1 medium onion, coarsely chopped
2 celery stalks, finely chopped

2 cups corn kernels

1 cup lima beans

1 cup sliced mushrooms

1 teaspoon dried oregano

1/4 cup chopped fresh parsley

salt to taste

freshly ground black pepper to taste

Cut the green beans into 1-inch pieces. Steam until they are bright green, tender, but still crisp, about 7 minutes. Set aside.

In a large skillet, melt the butter over moderate heat. Add the onion and celery and sauté, stirring often, until the onion is softened, about 5 minutes. Add the reserved green beans, corn, lima beans, mushrooms, oregano, and parsley. Season to taste with salt and black pepper. Cook, stirring often, until the mushrooms are cooked through, about 5 to 7 minutes longer.

Serves 4

Basic Succotash

The Narraganset Indians befriended the Pilgrims and taught them to make a simple stew of corn and beans called *msickquatasch*. Pronouncing the word as best they could, the Pilgrims called the dish succotash. Modern-day versions of the dish always call for corn and lima beans, often enriched with butter and cream—ingredients that were unknown to the Native Americans before the arrival of the Europeans. The problem with succotash is that many otherwise adventurous eaters detest lima beans. Try substituting an equivalent amount of cooked kidney or pinto beans.

4 tablespoons unsalted butter

1 1/2 cups cooked lima beans

2 cups corn kernels

2 tablespoons heavy cream

salt to taste

freshly ground black pepper to taste

Melt the butter in a skillet over moderate heat. Add the lima beans, corn kernels, and cream. Cook, stirring often, until the mixture is slightly thickened, about 5 minutes. Season to taste with salt and black pepper.

Serves 4

Succotash with Tomatoes

1 tablespoon unsalted butter
1 medium onion, finely chopped
1 large, ripe tomato, seeded and coarsely chopped
1/4 cup heavy cream
1/8 teaspoon ground nutmeg
salt to taste
freshly ground black pepper to taste
1 1/2 cups cooked lima beans
2 cups corn kernels

Melt the butter in a skillet over moderate heat. Add the onion and cook, stirring often, until the onion is softened, about 5 minutes. Add the tomato and cook, stirring often, until the tomato is softened, about 5 minutes longer.

Reduce the heat to low and add the cream and nutmeg to the skillet. Season to taste with salt and black pepper. Add the lima beans and corn and cook, stirring often, until the mixture is simmering hot. Serve at once.

Serves 4

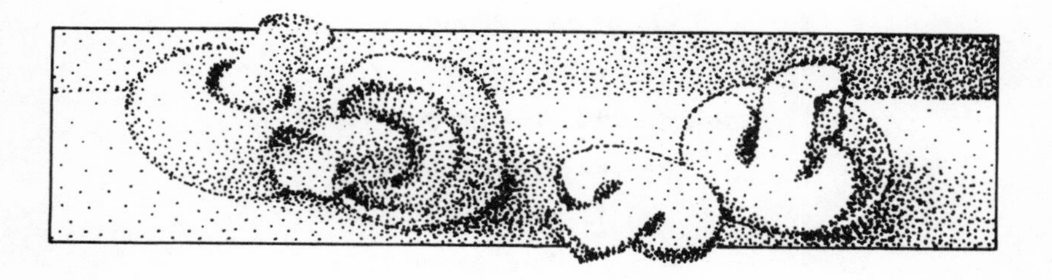

Makai (Corn Cooked with Milk)

A popular dish on the Indian subcontinent. It's unusual and quite spicy.

2 cups corn kernels
2 cups milk
1 teaspoon ground cumin
1/2 teaspoon finely chopped fresh ginger
1 hot green chili pepper, seeded and finely chopped
1/4 teaspoon cayenne pepper
2 tablespoons unsweetened grated coconut
1/4 cup chopped fresh cilantro

Combine the corn and milk in a saucepan and simmer over low heat, stirring often, until all but about 2 tablespoons of the milk has been absorbed. This should take about 15 minutes or less.

Add the cumin, ginger, chili pepper, cayenne pepper, coconut, and cilantro. Simmer, stirring often, 3 minutes longer.

Serves 4

Fried Green Tomatoes

Use only green tomatoes without any red on them to make this traditional Southern side dish.

3 large green tomatoes
salt to taste
freshly ground black pepper to taste
cayenne pepper to taste
1/3 cup flour
1/3 cup yellow cornmeal
1/4 cup vegetable oil

Cut the tomatoes into ¼-inch slices. Season the slices generously on both sides with salt, black pepper, and cayenne pepper.

Combine the flour and cornmeal in a mixing bowl. Dredge the tomato slices well in the mixture, shaking off any excess.

In a large, heavy skillet, heat the vegetable oil until it is very hot but not smoking. Add the tomato slices and sauté until golden brown on both sides, about 3 to 4 minutes per side. (Sauté the slices in batches if necessary.) Drain on paper towels and serve at once.

Serves 4

Corn-Stuffed Tomatoes

4 large, ripe tomatoes
3 tablespoons unsalted butter
1 small onion, finely chopped
1 cup corn kernels
1 cup crumbled stale cornbread
1 teaspoon dried basil
1 teaspoon dried oregano
salt to taste
freshly ground black pepper to taste
½ cup grated Parmesan cheese

Preheat the oven to 350°.

Core the tomatoes and scoop out the seeds. Set aside.

Melt the butter in a skillet. Add the onion and cook, stirring often, until the onion is softened, about 5 minutes. Add the corn kernels, cornbread crumbs, basil, oregano, and salt and black pepper to taste. Mix well.

Stuff the reserved tomato shells with the corn mixture and top with the Parmesan cheese. Place in a greased baking dish and bake for 35 to 40 minutes.

Serves 4

CORN MAQUECHOUX

There are probably as many recipes for maquechoux as there are Cajun cooks. This dish should be fairly dry; keep cooking and stirring until it is.

8 ears fresh corn, husked
4 tablespoons unsalted butter
6 scallions, thinly sliced
1 red bell pepper, seeded and chopped
2 large, ripe tomatoes, seeded and chopped
1/2 teaspoon sugar
1/4 teaspoon dried thyme
1/4 teaspoon dried basil
1/4 teaspoon cayenne pepper
1/2 cup heavy cream
salt to taste
freshly ground black pepper to taste

Using a sharp knife, cut the kernels from the ears. With the back of the knife, scrape the ears to remove the additional milk and corn bits from the cob. There should be about 4 cups of corn.

Melt the butter in a large, heavy skillet over moderate heat. Add the scallion and red pepper and cook, stirring often, until the pepper is softened, about 5 minutes.

Add the tomatoes, sugar, thyme, basil, and cayenne pepper. Cook, stirring occasionally, until the tomatoes are softened, about 5 minutes longer. Add the reserved corn and the cream and cook, stirring constantly, until the mixture is quite thick and almost dry, about 10 to 15 minutes. Season with salt and black pepper to taste.

Serves 4

Corn and Eggplant Casserole

1 medium eggplant, peeled and diced
1 cup water
3 tablespoons unsalted butter
2 tablespoons olive oil
1 large onion, finely chopped
1 cup corn kernels
1 egg
1/4 cup finely chopped green bell pepper
1 large garlic clove, finely chopped
1/4 teaspoon salt
1/4 teaspoon cayenne pepper
freshly ground black pepper to taste
1 cup shredded Cheddar cheese
1/2 cup plain breadcrumbs

Place the eggplant and water in a saucepan, cover, and bring to boil. Reduce the heat and simmer until the eggplant is tender, about 20 minutes. Drain well, reserving 1/2 cup of the cooking liquid.

Preheat the oven to 350°.

Melt the butter with the oil in a large saucepan over moderate heat. Add half the onion and cook, stirring often, until the onion is browned, about 8 minutes. Remove the onions from the saucepan and set aside. Add the corn kernels to the saucepan and cook, stirring often, until the corn is thoroughly heated through, about 5 minutes. Return the reserved cooked onions to the saucepan. Add the remaining onion, the reserved eggplant, and the egg, green pepper, garlic, salt, cayenne pepper, and lots of black pepper. Stir well and add half the cheese, half the breadcrumbs, and the reserved eggplant cooking liquid. Mix well.

Pour the mixture into an ungreased 8-inch baking dish. Smooth the top and sprinkle it with the remaining cheese, topped with the remaining breadcrumbs. Bake until the cheese is melted and the casserole bubbles, about 30 to 40 minutes. Let stand 10 minutes before serving.

Serves 4

WILD RICE WITH CORN

Two important Native American foods—wild rice and corn—are combined in this interesting dish. Cook the wild rice as directed on the package, taking care not to overcook it.

2 tablespoons unsalted butter
2 tablespoons olive oil
3 garlic cloves, finely chopped
3 cups corn kernels
2 cups cooked wild rice
3 tablespoons finely chopped sun-dried tomatoes
1/3 cup chopped fresh basil
salt to taste
freshly ground black pepper to taste

In a large skillet, melt the butter with the olive oil over moderate heat. Add the garlic, corn, wild rice, and tomatoes. Cook, stirring often, until the corn is thoroughly heated, about 4 minutes. Add the basil and season to taste with salt and black pepper. Serve at once.

Serves 4

CHEROKEE BEAN CAKES

3 cups cooked black beans, mashed
1 1/2 cups cornmeal
1 teaspoon salt
3/4 cup milk
2 eggs
1/2 cup vegetable oil

In a mixing bowl, combine the black beans, cornmeal, salt, milk, and eggs. Mix well to form a stiff dough. Divide the dough into 4 portions and form each into a cake about 3 inches in diameter.

Heat the oil in a large, heavy skillet. Add the bean cakes and cook until they are lightly browned all over, about 2 to 3 minutes per side. Drain on paper towels.

Serves 4

Humitas (South American Corn Puree)

Basically just a simple corn puree flavored with Parmesan cheese, this dish is popular throughout South America.

3 cups corn kernels
1/2 cup milk
2 eggs
1/2 teaspoon sugar
2 jalapeño peppers, seeded and finely chopped
salt to taste
freshly ground black pepper to taste
2 to 3 tablespoons unsalted butter
1 onion, finely chopped
2 tablespoons finely chopped red bell pepper
3/4 cup grated Parmesan cheese

In a food processor or blender, puree the corn kernels with the milk, eggs, sugar, jalapeño peppers, and salt and black pepper to taste. Set aside.

Melt the butter in a skillet over moderate heat. Add the onion and red pepper and cook until the vegetables are softened, about 5 minutes. Add the reserved corn puree and continue to cook, stirring often, until the mixture is slightly thickened and very hot. Remove from the heat and stir in the Parmesan cheese.

Serves 4

Scrapple

The thrifty Pennsylvania Dutch waste nothing from a hog butchering. Scrapple will keep for weeks in the refrigerator (do not freeze). Slices of this highly seasoned, caseless sausage are traditionally fried in a skillet until crispy on the outside and served with maple syrup or molasses as a side dish at breakfast.

3 cups finely ground pork
6 cups beef broth
6 cups water
2 teaspoons salt
2 teaspoons coarsely ground black pepper
½ teaspoon cayenne pepper
1 teaspoon dried sage
1 teaspoon dried basil
½ teaspoon dried rosemary
½ teaspoon ground thyme
3½ cups cornmeal

Place the pork, beef broth, and water in a 6-quart pot and bring the liquid to a boil. Reduce the heat to low and simmer, occasionally skimming off the fat, for 20 minutes. Add the salt, black pepper, cayenne pepper, sage, basil, rosemary, and thyme and raise the heat to moderate.

When the mixture returns to a rolling boil, slowly whisk in the cornmeal, stirring often to break up any lumps. Reduce the heat to low again and simmer the mixture, stirring frequently, until it has a thick, mushlike consistency, about 1 hour.

Pour the mixture into 3 greased 8- or 9-inch loaf pans. Let cool, cover with waxed paper, and refrigerate until ready to use.

Makes 3 loaves

CHAPTER
5

Spoonbreads and Puddings

Spoonbread is basically a baked mixture of cornmeal, eggs, and cream (often with additional ingredients), served as a side dish. The name may come from the Native Americans, who made a sort of porridge called suppawn. *Others claim that the dish originated when a careless cook added too much water to the cornbread batter, ending up with a concoction that was eaten directly from the dish with a spoon. In any case, spoonbread is really much more like a custard or soufflé than a bread.* ❧ *It makes a good accompaniment to roasts, grilled meats, and very spicy dishes, and is an interesting alternative to mashed potatoes.*

Corn puddings use corn kernels, not cornmeal, as their base. ❧ *They are otherwise similar to spoonbreads.*

To make individual servings of spoonbread or corn pudding, spoon the batter into greased 1-cup baking dishes or large muffin tins and bake until puffed and golden brown on top—generally about 18 to 20 minutes.

Basic Spoonbread I

Any basic spoonbread can be enlivened by adding ingredients such as chopped ham, shrimp pieces, chopped scallions, shredded cheese, and the like—individually or in combination—to the cornmeal batter before adding the egg whites.

2 cups water
1 teaspoon salt
2 tablespoons unsalted butter
1 cup yellow cornmeal
3 eggs, separated
1 cup milk

Preheat the oven to 400°.

In a 2-quart saucepan over moderate heat, bring the water, salt, and butter to a boil. Slowly whisk in the cornmeal. When the mixture returns to a simmer, remove the saucepan from the heat. Whisk in the egg yolks and milk.

In another bowl, beat the egg whites until they are stiff but not dry. Fold the egg whites into the cornmeal mixture.

Fold the cornmeal mixture into a well-greased 2-quart baking or soufflé dish. Bake until golden brown and puffed on top, about 35 to 40 minutes. Serve at once.

Serves 4

Basic Spoonbread II

1 cup yellow cornmeal
3 cups milk
1 teaspoon salt
1 teaspoon baking powder
3 tablespoons unsalted butter
3 eggs, separated

Preheat the oven to 400°.

In a large mixing bowl, beat together the cornmeal and 1 cup of the milk. Stir well to break up any lumps.

In a heavy, 2-quart saucepan, bring the remaining 2 cups of milk just to a boil over low heat and immediately remove from the heat. Slowly stir the hot milk into the cornmeal mixture.

Pour the cornmeal mixture back into the saucepan. Add the salt, baking powder, and butter and cook over low heat, stirring constantly, until the mixture is smooth and thickened, about 10 to 15 minutes.

Remove the saucepan from the heat and let the mixture cool for 5 minutes. Beat in the egg yolks.

In another bowl, beat the egg whites until they are stiff but not dry. Fold them into the cornmeal mixture.

Fold the cornmeal mixture into a well-greased 2-quart baking or soufflé dish. Bake until golden brown and puffed on top, about 45 to 50 minutes. Serve at once.

Serves 4

Spoonbread with Peas

An extremely rich and very satisfying dish.

10 ounces thawed frozen peas
1/4 cup heavy cream
2 cups light cream
4 tablespoons unsalted butter
1 tablespoon honey
1 cup yellow cornmeal
4 eggs, separated
1 teaspoon baking powder
1/4 teaspoon hot pepper sauce
salt to taste
freshly ground black pepper to taste

Preheat the oven to 375°.

In a food processor or blender, combine the peas and heavy cream. Process breifly just until the peas are finely chopped but not pureed. Set aside.

In a 2-quart saucepan over low heat, combine the light cream, butter, and honey. Cook until the butter just melts. Slowly whisk in the cornmeal. Cook, stirring constantly, until the mixture is thickened and smooth, about 3 to 4 minutes. Pour the cornmeal mixture into a large mixing bowl and let cool for 5 minutes.

Stir in the egg yolks one by one. Stir in the reserved pea mixture, the baking powder, and the hot pepper sauce. Season to taste with salt and lots of black pepper.

In another bowl, beat the egg whites until they are stiff but not dry. Fold them into the cornmeal mixture.

Fold the cornmeal mixture into a well-greased 2-quart baking or soufflé dish. Bake until golden brown and puffed on top, about 35 to 40 minutes. Serve at once.

Serves 6

Buttermilk Spoonbread

1 cup water
1 cup yellow cornmeal
3 tablespoons unsalted butter, melted
1 cup shredded mild Cheddar or Monterey Jack cheese
salt to taste
freshly ground black pepper to taste
1 cup buttermilk
3 eggs, separated
1 cup corn kernels

Preheat the oven to 375°.

In a 2-quart saucepan over moderate heat, bring the water to a boil. Quickly whisk in the cornmeal, reduce the heat to low, and cook, stirring constantly, until the mixture is thickened and smooth, about 10 minutes.

Remove the saucepan from the heat. Stir in the butter and cheese and season to taste with salt and black pepper. Beat in the buttermilk a little at a time, stirring constantly until it is all absorbed.

In a small bowl beat the egg yolks together. Stir the yolks into the cornmeal mixture. Stir in the corn kernels.

In another bowl, beat the egg whites until they are stiff but not dry. Fold them into the cornmeal mixture.

Fold the cornmeal mixture into a well-greased 2-quart baking or soufflé dish. Bake until golden brown and puffed on top, about 50 to 55 minutes. Serve at once.

Serves 4

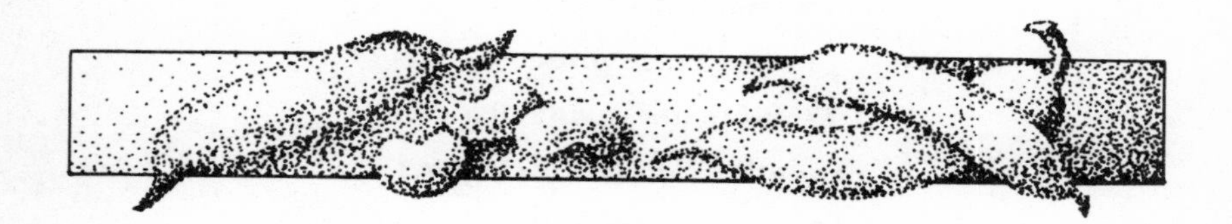

Basic Corn Pudding

As with spoonbreads, additional ingredients such as chopped fresh herbs, grated cheese, and the like may be added. For a sweeter pudding, leave out the black and cayenne pepper and add a teaspoon of sugar or a tablespoon of molasses, honey, or maple syrup.

3 eggs
2 cups heavy cream
3 tablespoons unsalted butter, melted
1/2 teaspoon salt
freshly ground black pepper to taste
1/8 teaspoon cayenne pepper
4 cups corn kernels

Preheat the oven to 350°.

In a large mixing bowl, beat the eggs. Add the cream, butter, salt, black pepper to taste, and cayenne. Beat well. Add the corn kernels and mix well.

Pour the corn mixture into a buttered 1 1/2-quart baking dish. Place the dish in a larger pan. Add enough hot water to the pan to come halfway up the sides of the baking dish. Bake until the pudding is lightly browned on top and a knife inserted into the center comes out clean, about 35 to 40 minutes.

Serves 6

Creamed Corn Pudding

2 eggs
2 tablespoons unsalted butter, melted
2 cups milk
1 17-ounce can cream-style corn
1 small onion, finely chopped
1 teaspoon salt
freshly ground black pepper to taste

Preheat the oven to 325°.

In a large mixing bowl, beat the eggs. Add the butter and milk and beat well. Add the cream-style corn, onion, salt, and black pepper to taste. Mix well.

Pour the corn mixture into a buttered 1½-quart baking dish. Place the dish in a larger pan. Add enough hot water to the pan to come halfway up the sides of the baking dish. Bake until the pudding is lightly browned on top and a knife inserted into the center comes out clean, about 50 to 60 minutes.

Serves 6

Confetti Corn Pudding

2 tablespoons unsalted butter
1 medium onion, finely chopped
1 green bell pepper, seeded and finely chopped
1 red bell pepper, seeded and finely chopped
1 celery stalk, finely chopped
1 carrot, finely chopped
4 cups corn kernels
2 cups light cream
½ teaspoon salt
freshly ground black pepper to taste
dash cayenne pepper
¼ teaspoon ground nutmeg
2 eggs
1 tablespoon flour

Preheat the oven to 350°.

Melt the butter in a large saucepan over moderate heat. Add the onion, green pepper, red pepper, celery, and carrot. Cook, stirring often, until the onion is softened, about 5 minutes.

Add the corn, cream, salt, black pepper to taste, cayenne pepper, and nutmeg.

Simmer, stirring occasionally, until the mixture is slightly thickened, about 10 minutes. Remove the saucepan from the heat and let cool for 10 minutes.

In a bowl, beat the eggs. Whisk in the flour. Stir the egg mixture into the corn mixture and blend well.

Pour the mixture into a buttered 2-quart baking dish. Bake until the pudding is lightly browned on top and a knife inserted into the center comes out clean, about 30 to 35 minutes. Let stand for 5 minutes before serving.

Serves 6

Corn and Tomato Pudding

This interesting dish comes from Ecuador.

2 cups corn kernels
1 cup shredded Muenster or Monterey Jack cheese
4 tablespoons unsalted butter
salt to taste
freshly ground black pepper to taste
6 eggs
3 large, ripe tomatoes, seeded and finely chopped
3 tablespoons chopped fresh cilantro

Preheat the oven to 350°.

In a food processor, puree the corn kernels, cheese, and butter together. Season to taste with salt and black pepper. Add the eggs one at a time, processing briefly after each addition.

Pour the corn puree into a mixing bowl and stir in the tomatoes and cilantro.

Pour the mixture into a buttered 1½-quart baking dish. Bake until the pudding is lightly browned on top and a knife inserted into the center comes out clean, about 55 to 60 minutes.

Serves 4

TEX-MEX CORN PUDDING

1 tablespoon unsalted butter
1 small onion, finely chopped
1/4 cup finely chopped green bell pepper
1/4 cup finely chopped canned green chilies
1 jalapeño pepper, seeded and finely chopped
1 1/2 cups corn kernels
1 1/2 tablespoons flour
1/2 cup milk
3 eggs
1 cup heavy cream
1/2 teaspoon salt
freshly ground black pepper to taste
1/4 teaspoon ground nutmeg
1/8 teaspoon ground allspice
2 cups shredded mild Cheddar or Monterey Jack cheese

Preheat the oven to 350°.

Melt the butter in a large skillet over moderate heat. Add the onion and green pepper. Cook, stirring often, until the onion is softened, about 5 minutes. Add the green chilies, jalapeño pepper, and 1 cup of the corn kernels. Cook, stirring often, until all the vegetables are softened, about 10 minutes longer.

In a food processor or blender, combine the remaining 1/2 cup corn kernels with the flour and milk. Process until pureed.

In a large mixing bowl, beat the eggs well. Add the corn puree and the cream, salt, lots of black pepper, nutmeg, and allspice. Mix well. Add the corn mixture from the skillet and the cheese and mix well again.

Pour the corn mixture into a buttered 1 1/2-quart baking dish. Place the dish in a larger pan. Add enough hot water to the pan to come halfway up the sides of the baking dish. Bake until the pudding is firm and lightly browned on top and a knife inserted into the center comes out clean, about 55 to 60 minutes. Let stand 15 minutes before serving.

Serves 6

SHRIMP AND CORN PUDDING

2 pounds cooked shrimp, shelled and cut into thirds
6 cups corn kernels
4 tablespoons unsalted butter
1 small onion, finely chopped
3 eggs
1 teaspoon salt
freshly ground black pepper to taste
1/8 teaspoon ground mace
1 cup heavy cream

Preheat the oven to 300°.

In a mixing bowl, combine the shrimp and corn kernels.

Melt the butter in a large skillet over moderate heat. Add the onion and cook, stirring often, until the onion is softened, about 5 minutes. Add the onion to the shrimp and corn.

In another bowl, beat the eggs with the salt, lots of black pepper, mace, and cream. Add the mixture to the shrimp and corn.

Pour the corn mixture into a buttered 2-quart baking dish. Cover the dish and bake until the pudding is firm, about 40 to 50 minutes. Remove the cover and bake until the pudding is nicely browned on top, about 10 minutes longer.

Serves 6

CREAMY CORNBREAD PUDDING

2/3 cup milk
2 eggs
6 tablespoons unsalted butter, melted
1 teaspoon baking powder
1/2 teaspoon baking soda
1/2 teaspoon salt

freshly ground black pepper to taste
1 cup cornmeal
1 17-ounce can cream-style corn
2 4-ounce cans green chilies, finely chopped
2 cups shredded mild Cheddar or Monterey Jack cheese

Preheat the oven to 400°.

In a large mixing bowl, beat together the milk, eggs, melted butter, baking powder, baking soda, salt, and lots of black pepper. Mix in the cornmeal and cream-style corn and stir well.

Spread half the batter in a greased 2-quart baking dish. Cover the batter with half the chopped green chilies and half the cheese. Pour the remaining batter over the cheese and top with the remaining chilies and cheese.

Bake until the mixture is browned around the edges and set in the middle, about 40 to 45 minutes. Let stand for 5 minutes before serving.

Serves 6

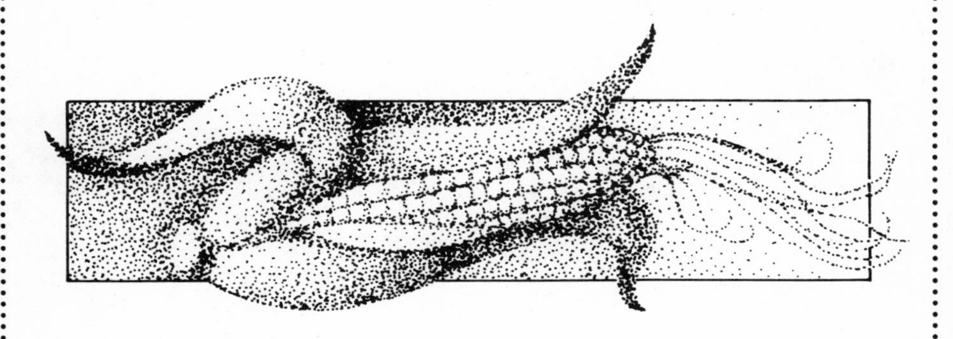

CHAPTER

6

Polenta

Cornmeal cooked with liquid into a thick porridge is the oldest and simplest cornmeal dish. ✂ *Known as mush to Americans, polenta to Italians,* mamaliga *to Rumanians,* puliszka *to Hungarians, and* ugali *or* posho *to Africans, cornmeal forms a versatile, nutritious base for a wide and delicious range of additional ingredients.* ✂ *For the most attractive dish, use yellow cornmeal.*

Cornmeal Mush

In colonial times, cornmeal mush—also called stirabout pudding or hasty pudding—was often served for supper, topped with fresh milk and sometimes molasses or maple syrup. Today cornmeal mush is still as simple and as satisfying as it was then. Pack leftover mush into a loaf pan, chill it overnight, and serve slices, fried lightly in butter, for breakfast.

6 cups water
1 teaspoon salt
1 cup yellow cornmeal

In a heavy, 2-quart saucepan, bring the water and salt to a rapid boil. Slowly whisk in the cornmeal, stirring constantly to break up any lumps. Bring the mixture to a boil again, then reduce the heat to very low. Cook, stirring often with a long-handled wooden spoon, until very thick, about 35 to 45 minutes.

Serves 4

Cush-Cush

Sometimes spelled couche-couche, this is the Cajun version of cornmeal mush. A cast-iron skillet is essential for getting the delicious bottom crust. In Cajun country, this is served in bowls for breakfast, topped with cane syrup.

2 cups yellow cornmeal
1 teaspoon salt
1⅔ cups hot water
4 tablespoons vegetable oil

Place the cornmeal and salt in a large mixing bowl. Gradually add 1⅓ cups of the water, stirring constantly to break up any lumps.

In a 9-inch cast-iron skillet, heat the oil over moderate heat until it is quite hot, about 4 minutes. Add the cornmeal mixture, spreading it evenly over the bottom of the skillet. Cook without stirring until a thick, well-browned crust forms on the bottom of the skillet, about 6 to 7 minutes (reduce the heat if the mixture seems likely to burn).

Using a spatula, turn the mixture over in batches. Pour the remaining ⅓ cup water over the top and cook until the cornmeal is fluffy, about 3 to 4 minutes longer. The mixture will still be quite moist. Serve at once.

Serves 4

Basic Polenta

Polenta, the Italian version of cornmeal mush, derives its name from the Latin word *pulmentum*, or porridge. It is excellent served straight from the stove with a sprinkling of Parmesan cheese. Seasonings and other ingredients such as onions, garlic, mushrooms, and so on are usually stirred into the mixture shortly before it has finished cooking. Polenta is usually prepared in advance, poured into a dish or loaf pan, and chilled. To serve, the solid polenta is then cut into slices or wedges and gently sautéed (for a delicious and unusual barbecue dish, try grilling polenta). For a more elaborate dish, spoon any sort of gravy or pasta sauce over the sautéed polenta.

6½ cups water
1 teaspoon salt
2 cups yellow cornmeal

In a heavy 2-quart saucepan, bring the water to a rapid boil over high heat. Reduce the heat to moderate. Stir in the salt. Pour in the cornmeal in a thin, steady stream, stirring constantly with a long-handled wooden spoon.

Continue to cook, stirring constantly, until the mixture is smooth and thick and begins to pull away from the sides of the saucepan, about 15 to 20 minutes.

Serves 4

Quick Basic Polenta

5 cups milk
1½ cups yellow cornmeal

In a heavy, 2-quart saucepan, bring the milk to a boil over moderate heat (do not let the milk scorch). Pour in the cornmeal in a thin, steady stream, stirring constantly with a long-handled wooden spoon.

Continue to cook, stirring constantly, until the mixture is smooth and thick and begins to pull away from the sides of the saucepan, about 5 minutes.

Serves 4

Basic Polenta in the Microwave

Add cheese, black pepper, or other ingredients just after removing the dish from the microwave oven.

4 cups cold water
1 teaspoon salt
1¼ cups yellow cornmeal

Combine the water, salt, and cornmeal in a large microwave-safe serving dish. Stir well to break up any lumps. Microwave at full power, uncovered, for 7 minutes. Stir well, cover with a paper towel, and microwave 7 minutes longer. Stir well again and microwave, uncovered, for 3 minutes. Remove from the oven and let stand for 5 minutes. Stir well again before serving.

Serves 4

Ugali (African Cornmeal Porridge)

Cornmeal cooked into a thick porridge is a staple food in many parts of sub-Saharan Africa. The Swahili word for the dish is *posho.* It is called *ugali* in Kenya and Tanzania, *nsima* in Malawi and Zambia, *putu* or *pap* in South Africa, and *oshifima* in Namibia. It's best made with white cornmeal. Ugali is generally served by placing it in the center of the table. Diners pull off small chunks, flatten them, and use the ugali to scoop up stew or condiments.

1 cup water
1 teaspoon salt
1 cup milk
1 cup white cornmeal

In a heavy 2-quart saucepan, bring the water and salt to a boil.

In a mixing bowl, stir the milk into the cornmeal until smooth. Slowly pour the mixture into the boiling water, stirring constantly with a long-handled wooden spoon. Reduce the heat to very low and cook, stirring often from the bottom, until the mixture is very stiff and pulls away from the sides of the saucepan, about 10 to 15 minutes.

Serves 4

Polenta with Four Cheeses

6½ cups water
1 teaspoon salt
2 cups yellow cornmeal
1 cup milk
4 tablespoons unsalted butter
½ cup shredded Muenster cheese
½ cup shredded Swiss cheese
½ cup shredded sharp Cheddar cheese
4 tablespoons grated Parmesan cheese

In a heavy 2-quart saucepan, bring the water to a rapid boil over high heat. Reduce the heat to moderate. Stir in the salt. Pour in the cornmeal in a thin, steady stream, stirring constantly with a long-handled wooden spoon.

Continue to cook, stirring constantly, until the mixture is smooth and thick and begins to pull away from the sides of the saucepan, about 15 to 20 minutes.

Add the milk and cook, stirring often, until it is absorbed, about 5 minutes longer.

Add the butter and Muenster, Swiss, and Cheddar cheeses. Cook, stirring often, until the cheeses have melted.

Pour the polenta into a serving dish and sprinkle with the Parmesan cheese. Let stand 10 minutes before serving.

Serves 4

Pecan Polenta

4 tablespoons unsalted butter
1 cup coarsely chopped pecans
3 cups water
3 cups chicken broth
1 teaspoon salt
2 cups yellow cornmeal
1/4 teaspoon ground nutmeg
freshly ground black pepper to taste

Melt 1 tablespoon of the butter in a skillet over moderate heat. Add the chopped pecans and cook until the pecans are lightly browned. Set aside.

In a heavy 2-quart saucepan, bring the water and chicken broth to a rapid boil over high heat. Reduce the heat to moderate. Stir in the salt. Pour in the cornmeal in a thin, steady stream, stirring constantly with a long-handled wooden spoon.

Continue to cook, stirring constantly, until the mixture is smooth and thick and begins to pull away from the sides of the saucepan, about 15 to 20 minutes. Stir in the nutmeg and black pepper to taste.

Remove the saucepan from the heat and stir in the reserved pecans. Spread the polenta in a greased, shallow baking dish and let cool for at least 1 hour (if refrigerated, this dish can be prepared up to 24 hours in advance).

Cut the cooled polenta into small squares.

Melt the remaining 3 tablespoons of butter in a large, heavy skillet over moderate heat. Add the polenta squares (in batches if necessary) and cook until lightly browned on both sides.

Serves 4

POLENTA WITH CORN

2½ cups milk
1 cup chicken broth
1 cup yellow cornmeal
1 cup corn kernels
¾ teaspoon salt
1½ tablespoons unsalted butter, melted
1½ tablespoons grated Parmesan cheese

In a heavy, 2-quart saucepan over moderate heat, bring the milk and chicken broth to a boil. Slowly whisk in the cornmeal, stirring constantly to break up any lumps. Cook, stirring constantly, until the mixture is thickened and smooth, about 15 minutes.

Remove the saucepan from the heat and stir in the corn kernels and salt. Pour the mixture into a greased, shallow baking dish and let cool for at least 1 hour (if refrigerated, this dish can be prepared up to 24 hours in advance).

Preheat the oven to 375°.

Brush the top of the polenta with the melted butter and sprinkle with the Parmesan cheese. Bake for 15 minutes. Let stand 10 minutes before serving.

Serves 4

Polenta with Leeks

5 large leeks
6 tablespoons unsalted butter
2 tablespoons olive oil
1/4 cup dry white wine
1/8 teaspoon ground cloves
1/8 teaspoon ground mace
2 1/2 cups milk
3/4 cup yellow cornmeal
4 tablespoons shredded Fontina cheese
salt to taste
freshly ground black pepper to taste

Discard the green parts from the leeks. Rinse the white parts well to remove all grit, pat dry, and chop finely.

Melt 2 tablespoons of the butter with the olive oil in a large, heavy skillet over moderate heat. Add the leeks and cook, stirring often, until softened, about 4 minutes. Add the wine, cloves, and mace and cook, stirring often, until the leeks are very tender, about 15 minutes longer. Raise the heat and continue to cook until all the liquid is gone. Set the leeks aside.

In a heavy, 2-quart saucepan, bring the milk to a boil over moderate heat. Pour in the cornmeal in a thin, steady stream, stirring constantly with a long-handled wooden spoon.

Continue to cook, stirring constantly, until the mixture is smooth and thick and begins to pull away from the sides of the saucepan, about 5 minutes. Stir in the reserved leeks and 2 tablespoons of the cheese. Season to taste with salt and black pepper.

Pour the mixture into a greased, shallow baking dish and let cool for at least 1 hour (if refrigerated, this dish can be prepared up to 24 hours in advance).

Preheat the oven to 375°.

Melt the remaining 4 tablespoons of butter. Brush the top of the polenta with the melted butter and sprinkle with the remaining 2 tablespoons cheese. Bake for 15 minutes. Let stand for 10 minutes before serving.

Serves 4

POLENTA WITH MUSHROOMS

If you can't find fresh shiitake mushrooms, substitute regular white mushrooms.

4 tablespoons unsalted butter
1 tablespoon olive oil
1 medium onion, finely chopped
2 garlic cloves, finely chopped
1/4 pound shiitake mushrooms
2 1/2 cups milk
3/4 cup yellow cornmeal
4 tablespoons grated Parmesan cheese
1/2 teaspoon dried thyme
1/4 teaspoon hot red pepper flakes
salt to taste
freshly ground black pepper to taste
2 tablespoons unsalted butter, melted

Heat the olive oil in a large, heavy skillet over moderate heat. Add the onions and garlic and cook, stirring often, until the onions are softened, about 5 minutes. Add the mushrooms and cook, stirring constantly, until the mushrooms are golden and any liquid has evaporated. Set aside.

In a heavy, 2-quart saucepan, bring the milk to a boil over moderate heat. Pour in the cornmeal in a thin, steady stream, stirring constantly with a long-handled wooden spoon.

Continue to cook, stirring constantly, until the mixture is smooth and thick and begins to pull away from the sides of the saucepan, about 5 minutes. Stir in 2 tablespoons of the cheese and the thyme and hot red pepper flakes. Stir in the reserved mushroom mixture. Season to taste with salt and black pepper.

Pour the mixture into a greased, shallow baking dish and let cool for at least 1 hour (if refrigerated, this dish can be prepared up to 24 hours in advance).

Preheat the oven to 375°.

Brush the top of the polenta with the melted butter and sprinkle with the remaining 2 tablespoons cheese. Bake for 15 minutes. Let stand for 10 minutes before serving.

Serves 4

Polenta with Sausage

1 tablespoon olive oil
1 small onion, finely chopped
1 small green bell pepper, seeded and finely chopped
1 cup corn kernels
½ pound hot Italian sausage,
removed from casing and coarsely chopped
1 cup chicken broth
1½ cups water
¾ cup yellow cornmeal
½ teaspoon dried oregano
½ teaspoon dried basil
salt to taste
freshly ground black pepper to taste
1 tablespoon grated Parmesan cheese

Heat the oil in a skillet over moderate heat. Add the onion, green pepper, and corn kernels and cook, stirring often, until the onion is softened, about 5 minutes. Raise the heat to high and add the sausage. Cook, stirring often, until the sausage is cooked through, about 5 minutes. Set aside.

In a heavy, 2-quart saucepan, bring the chicken broth and water to a boil over moderate heat. Pour in the cornmeal in a thin, steady stream, stirring constantly with a long-handled wooden spoon.

Continue to cook, stirring constantly, until the mixture is smooth and thick and begins to pull away from the sides of the saucepan, about 5 minutes. Add the reserved sausage mixture along with the oregano and basil. Season to taste with salt and black pepper.

Pour the mixture into a greased, shallow baking dish and let cool for at least 1 hour (if refrigerated, this dish can be prepared up to 24 hours in advance).

Preheat the oven to 375°.

Sprinkle the top of the polenta with the cheese. Bake for 15 minutes. Let stand for 10 minutes before serving.

Serves 4

Polenta and Greens Casserole

6½ cups water
1 teaspoon salt
2 cups yellow cornmeal
½ cup grated Romano cheese
4 slices bacon, coarsely chopped
2 tablespoons olive oil
2 garlic cloves, finely chopped
3 cups coarsely chopped arugula
3 cups coarsely chopped fresh spinach
salt to taste
freshly ground black pepper to taste
1 cup shredded Fontina cheese

In a heavy 2-quart saucepan, bring the water to a rapid boil over high heat. Reduce the heat to moderate. Stir in the salt. Pour in the cornmeal in a thin, steady stream, stirring constantly with a long-handled wooden spoon.

Continue to cook, stirring constantly, until the mixture is smooth and thick and begins to pull away from the sides of the saucepan, about 15 to 20 minutes. Stir in the Romano cheese and set aside.

Preheat the oven to 450°.

In a skillet with a lid, sauté the bacon pieces over moderate heat until crisp, about 6 to 7 minutes. Remove with a slotted spoon and set aside.

Add 1 tablespoon olive oil to the bacon grease. Add the garlic, arugula, and spinach and season to taste with salt and lots of black pepper. Cover the skillet tightly and cook over moderate heat until the greens are wilted, about 5 minutes.

Remove the greens from the skillet with a slotted spoon. Drain briefly in a colander, then finely chop the greens.

Using about a third of the polenta, make a layer in the bottom of a greased loaf pan. Use half the chopped greens to make another layer. Top with half the reserved bacon and ⅓ cup of the Fontina cheese. Use another third of the polenta to make another layer. Top with the remaining greens, then the remaining bacon, and then all but 2 tablespoons of the remaining Fontina. Use the last of the polenta to make another layer. Brush with the remaining 1 tablespoon olive oil and sprinkle with the remaining Fontina.

Bake until the casserole is lightly browned on top, about 15 minutes. Let stand 10 minutes before serving in slices.

Serves 4

Polenta and Eggplant Casserole

Use your favorite garlicky tomato sauce to make this casserole.

6½ cups water
1 teaspoon salt
2 cups yellow cornmeal
3 cups tomato sauce
2 medium eggplants, sliced into ½-inch rounds
¾ cup shredded mozzarella cheese
½ cup grated Parmesan cheese

In a heavy 2-quart saucepan, bring the water to a rapid boil over high heat. Reduce the heat to moderate. Stir in the salt. Pour in the cornmeal in a thin, steady stream, stirring constantly with a long-handled wooden spoon.

Continue to cook, stirring constantly, until the mixture is smooth and thick and begins to pull away from the sides of the saucepan, about 15 to 20 minutes.

Pour the mixture into a greased loaf pan and chill overnight.

Preheat the oven to 375°.

Cut the polenta into 1/2-inch slices. Arrange half the slices in a layer in the bottom of a greased, 9 × 13-inch baking dish. Arrange all the eggplant slices in a layer on top of the polenta. Spread 2 cups of the tomato sauce over the eggplant. Arrange the remaining polenta slices in a layer on top of the tomato sauce. Cover with the remaining tomato sauce and sprinkle evenly with the mozzarella and Parmesan cheese. Cover the dish and bake until the cheese is browned and the eggplant is tender, about 45 minutes.

Serves 4

Mamaliga with Cheese

Mamaliga is the Rumanian version of cornmeal mush. For all intents and purposes, it is identical to polenta, although in Eastern Europe mamaliga is often enriched with dairy products. This version calls for feta cheese and sour cream.

4 cups water
1 cup yellow cornmeal
1 teaspoon salt
3 tablespoons unsalted butter
1 cup crumbled feta cheese
1 teaspoon dried dill
freshly ground black pepper to taste
½ cup sour cream

Preheat the oven to 375°.

In a heavy, 2-quart saucepan, bring the water to a rapid boil over high heat. Reduce the heat to moderate. Stir in the salt. Pour in the cornmeal in a thin, steady stream, stirring constantly with a long-handled wooden spoon.

Continue to cook, stirring constantly, until the mixture is smooth and thick and begins to pull away from the sides of the saucepan, about 15 to 20 minutes.

Stir in the butter, feta cheese, and dill. Season to taste with lots of black pepper. Spread the mixture in a greased baking dish and top with the sour cream. Bake until lightly browned on top, about 15 minutes.

Serves 4

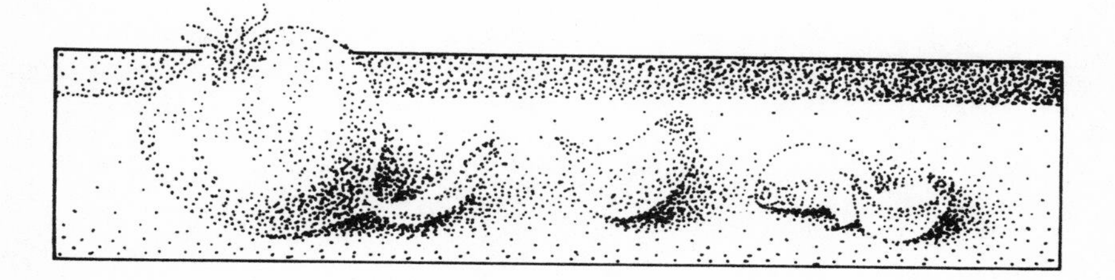

CHAPTER 7

Hominy and Grits

Centuries ago the Native Americans learned to boil stored kernels of dried corn in water mixed with wood ash. ❖ *This procedure loosened the tough, indigestible outer husk of the kernels, allowing it to be slipped off easily.* ❖ *More importantly, the alkaline wood ash increased the dietary availability of the niacin and other important nutrients in the corn.* ❖ *The Algonquian-speaking Native Americans of the Northeast called the soft, hulled corn kernels* rockahomonie or sagamite. *White settlers, especially those in the Southeast, eventually accepted the food as a staple and called it hominy, although the French settlers of Louisiana preferred to call it sac–*camité.

At one time, every housewife knew how to prepare her own hominy. The tedious process involved boiling the dried kernels in a lye solution, rinsing it in several changes of water, and removing the hulls by hand. No wonder the hominy street vendor was a common figure until early in the twentieth century, when he was supplanted by canned and (later) frozen hominy.

Because hominy was an inexpensive food associated with Southern and Mexican cuisine, in the minds of some it became a food of poverty, to be avoided whenever possible. Although it was once a staple found in every food market, canned hominy is hard to find today–and frozen hominy is almost impossible to find–in supermarkets outside of the South and Southwest. A trip to a specialty Hispanic food market may be needed.

Perhaps no other food is as closely associated with Southern cooking as grits. Made from dried hominy ground to a coarse meal, grits are unjustly ignored even by adventurous cooks, who will cheerfully experiment with arborio rice while neglecting corn. Grits are a traditional breakfast food but can also appear in many other guises as side dishes.

Finely ground dried hominy is called masa harina–literally, dough flour. Masa harina is used to make tortillas and many other dough-based dishes in Mexican and Latin American cuisine. It is not at all the same thing as cornmeal.

Hominy, grits, and masa harina are offered in both white and yellow versions. The difference is strictly visual—use whatever is available. Drain canned hominy and rinse well before adding to the recipe; thaw frozen hominy.

Basic Grits

Generally speaking, roughly 4 tablespoons of any kind of grits—regular, quick, or instant—cooked in 1 cup of water yields about 1 cup of cooked grits. Assume that an individual serving of grits is about 1 cup. Just how thick and creamy grits should be is a matter of personal preference. For thicker grits, use a little less water; for thinner grits, use a little more. Stone-ground grits preserve the germ and are both more flavorful and more nutritious, but take longer to cook.

4 cups water
½ teaspoon salt
1 cup grits

Bring the water to a rapid boil in a 2-quart saucepan over high heat. Add the salt. Pour in the grits in a steady stream, stirring constantly to break up any lumps. Reduce the heat to low and simmer, stirring often, until all the liquid is absorbed and the grits are thick and creamy, about 30 to 40 minutes.

Serves 4

Basic Quick Grits

Look in the hot cereal section of the supermarket to find grits. If you opt for the instant kind, cook according to the package directions.

4 cups water
1/2 teaspoon salt
1 cup quick grits

Bring the water to a rapid boil in a 2-quart saucepan over high heat. Add the salt. Pour in the grits in a steady stream, stirring constantly to break up any lumps. Reduce the heat to low and simmer, stirring often, until all the liquid is absorbed and the grits are thick and creamy, about 5 to 7 minutes.

Serves 4

MICROWAVE GRITS

Microwave ovens vary in power, so use the recipe below just as a guide. For some reason (probably having to do with particle physics), cooking grits in the microwave works well only when making a single portion. If you need more than a cup, use the stove-top method.

1 cup water
4 tablespoons grits
1/8 teaspoon salt

Put the water in a microwave-safe serving bowl (a 2-cup cereal bowl is perfect). Add the grits and salt and stir to break up any lumps. Microwave at half power (medium) for 7 minutes, then stir well. If the grits are not thick enough, microwave for another 2 to 3 minutes. Stir well before serving.

Serves 1

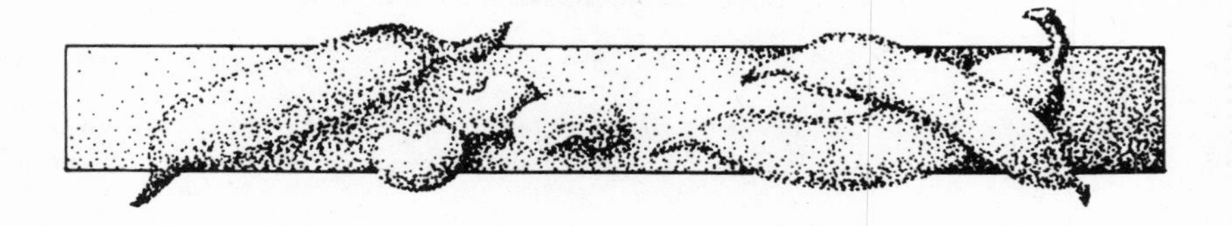

Fried Grits

This is not only the traditional way to use up leftover grits, it's the best.

4 cups cooked grits
1 tablespoon bacon drippings, unsalted butter, or vegetable oil

Pack the grits into a loaf pan. Cover and chill for several hours or overnight until grits are firm.

Turn the grits out of the pan and cut into ½-inch slices.

Heat the drippings in a large, heavy skillet over medium heat. Add the grits and cook until lightly browned on the bottom, about 7 to 10 minutes. Flip the slices over and cook on the other side until lightly browned, about 7 to 10 minutes longer.

Serves 4

Grits and Cheese Casserole

This classic Southern side dish goes perfectly with fried chicken, baked ham, or any roast. For a delicious smoky flavor, use 1 cup regular Cheddar cheese and ½ cup smoked Cheddar.

4 cups water
1 teaspoon salt
1 cup grits
2 eggs
1½ cups shredded Cheddar cheese
2 tablespoons unsalted butter
1 garlic clove, finely chopped
⅛ teaspoon cayenne pepper

Bring the water to a rapid boil in a 2-quart saucepan over high heat. Add the salt. Pour in the grits in a steady stream, stirring constantly to break up any lumps. Reduce the heat to low and simmer, stirring often, until all the liquid is absorbed and the grits are thick and creamy, about 30 to 40 minutes.

Preheat the oven to 350°.

Beat the eggs in a small mixing bowl. Beat in 2 tablespoons of the cooked grits, then add the mixture back to the saucepan and mix well. Add the cheese, butter, garlic, and cayenne pepper and mix well.

Pour the mixture into a greased 1½-quart baking dish and bake until the grits are firm and the top is lightly puffed, about 30 to 40 minutes. Let stand 5 minutes before serving.

Serves 4

Corny Grits Casserole

4 cups water
1 teaspoon salt
1 cup grits
2 eggs
1 cup shredded Cheddar cheese
1½ cups corn kernels
2 tablespoons unsalted butter
4 scallions, thinly sliced
1 green bell pepper, seeded and coarsely chopped
2 garlic cloves, finely chopped
⅛ teaspoon cayenne pepper
freshly ground black pepper to taste

Bring the water to a rapid boil in a 2-quart saucepan over high heat. Add the salt. Pour in the grits in a steady stream, stirring constantly to break up any lumps. Reduce the heat to low and simmer, stirring often, until all the liquid is absorbed and the grits are thick and creamy, about 30 to 40 minutes.

Preheat the oven to 350°.

Beat the eggs in a small mixing bowl. Beat in 2 tablespoons of the cooked grits, then add the mixture back to the saucepan and mix well. Add the cheese, corn, butter, scallions, green pepper, garlic, cayenne pepper, and black pepper and mix well.

Pour the mixture into a greased 2-quart baking dish and bake until the grits are firm and the top is lightly puffed, about 30 to 40 minutes. Let stand 5 minutes before serving.

Serves 4

Grits Casserole with Peas

1 tablespoon unsalted butter
1 tablespoon olive oil
1 medium onion, finely chopped
3 cups chicken broth
freshly ground black pepper to taste
1/2 teaspoon dried sage
1/2 teaspoon dried rosemary
1 cup grits
1/2 cup thawed frozen peas
1/4 cup fresh parsley, chopped
2 tablespoons grated Parmesan cheese

Melt the butter with the olive oil in a 2-quart saucepan over moderate heat. Add the onion and cook, stirring often, until softened, about 5 minutes. Add the chicken broth, black pepper, sage, and rosemary. Cook until the mixture comes to a boil, about 3 minutes.

Pour in the grits in a steady stream, stirring constantly to break up any lumps. Reduce the heat to low and simmer, stirring often, until almost all the liquid is absorbed and the grits are thickened, about 20 minutes. Add the peas, stir well, and cook 5 minutes longer.

Remove the saucepan from the heat and stir in the parsley and Parmesan cheese. Cover and let stand 10 minutes before serving.

Serves 4

AWENDAW

Awendaw (pronounced *ow endow,* with the accent on the first syllable), is a classic spoonbread from the low country of South Carolina.

2 tablespoons unsalted butter, softened
4 eggs, lightly beaten
2 cups cooked grits
1/8 teaspoon cayenne pepper
2 cups milk
1 cup cornmeal

Preheat the oven to 375°.

Combine the butter, eggs, grits, and cayenne pepper in a mixing bowl. Mix well. Slowly add the milk, stirring until it is all absorbed. Slowly add the cornmeal, stirring until it is all absorbed.

Pour the batter into a greased 1½-quart soufflé dish or deep baking dish. Bake until the mixture is firm and the top is lightly browned, about 45 to 50 minutes. Serve at once.

Serves 6

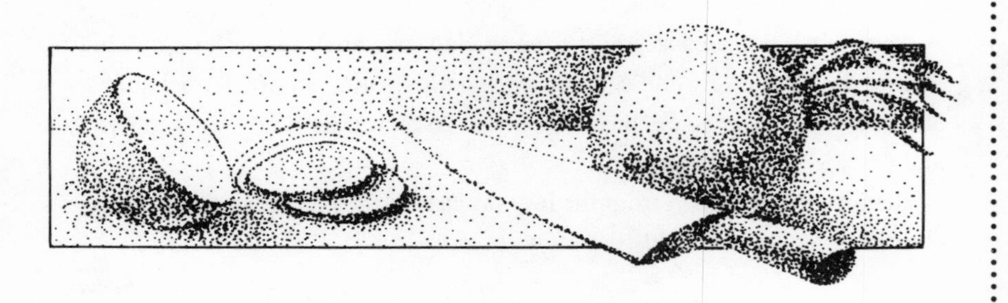

Hominy Soup

2 tablespoons vegetable oil
1 small onion, chopped
1 green bell pepper, seeded and coarsely chopped
2 garlic cloves, finely chopped
1 cup canned or frozen hominy
4 cups chicken broth
1 large, ripe tomato, seeded and chopped
¼ teaspoon hot red pepper flakes
½ teaspoon dried oregano
2 tablespoons lime juice
1 small zucchini, thinly sliced
½ cup coarsely chopped fresh cilantro

Heat the oil in a 2-quart saucepan over moderate heat. Add the onion, green pepper, and garlic and cook, stirring often, until the onion is softened, about 5 minutes.

Add the hominy, chicken broth, tomato, red pepper flakes, oregano, lime juice, zucchini, and cilantro. Lower the heat and simmer until the hominy is tender, about 20 to 30 minutes.

Serves 4

Hominy and Tortilla Soup

4 cups chicken broth
1 cup canned or frozen hominy
1 cup cooked pinto or kidney beans
2 dried chipotle peppers, seeded
½ cup coarsely chopped fresh cilantro
½ cup shredded Cheddar cheese

1 small tomato, seeded and diced
unsalted tortilla chips for garnish

Combine the chicken broth, hominy, beans, and chipotles in a 2-quart saucepan over medium heat. Cook until the mixture comes to a boil, then reduce the heat to low and simmer until the hominy is tender, about 20 to 30 minutes.

Stir in the cilantro.

Place about 1 cup of the soup and the chipotles in a food processor or blender and puree. Pour the mixture back into the soup, stir well, and cook until the soup is slightly thickened, about 5 minutes longer.

Divide the shredded cheese evenly among 4 individual serving bowls. Fill the bowls with soup and top with equal portions of the tomato. Garnish with tortilla chips.

Serves 4

Buttermilk Hominy Soup

This soup is a sort of hominy chowder.

4 bacon slices, coarsely chopped
1/2 cup finely chopped onion
1 cup canned or frozen hominy
2 cups buttermilk
1/2 teaspoon salt
freshly ground black pepper to taste
1 tablespoon chopped fresh dill

Cook the bacon in a heavy saucepan over medium heat until it just starts to brown, about 3 to 4 minutes. Add the onion and cook, stirring often, until softened, about 5 minutes longer. Add the hominy and cook, stirring occasionally, for 5 minutes.

Reduce the heat to low and add the buttermilk, salt, and black pepper. Cook, stirring occasionally, until the soup is hot, but do not let it boil. Sprinkle with the dill and serve warm.

Serves 4

Fried Hominy

A simple and satisfying side dish.

4 slices bacon, coarsely chopped
1 small onion, finely chopped
1 cup canned or frozen hominy
½ teaspoon salt
freshly ground black pepper to taste

Cook the bacon in a heavy saucepan over medium heat until it just starts to brown, about 3 to 4 minutes. Add the onion and cook, stirring often, until softened, about 5 minutes longer. Add the hominy, salt, and black pepper. Cook, stirring occasionally, for 5 minutes longer.

Serves 4

Hominy Hash

Serve this with thin slices of fried ham and corn muffins for brunch.

3 tablespoons bacon drippings or unsalted butter
2 cups canned or frozen hominy
4 scallions, thinly sliced
4 eggs, beaten
salt to taste
freshly ground black pepper to taste

Cook the bacon in a heavy skillet over medium heat until it just starts to brown, about 3 to 4 minutes. Add the hominy and scallions and cook, stirring often, until scallions are lightly browned, about 5 minutes longer. Season to taste with salt and black pepper. Pour the eggs evenly over the mixture and cook until eggs are set, about 7 to 8 minutes. Turn the egg mixture over, using a spatula, and cook until lightly browned on the other side.

Serves 4

Hominy Cakes

1 cup canned or frozen hominy
½ cup milk
1 egg
1 tablespoon unsalted butter, melted
½ teaspoon salt
1 teaspoon sugar
2 tablespoons unsalted butter

Preheat the oven to 375°.

Combine the hominy, milk, egg, melted butter, salt, and sugar in a food processor. Process until the mixture forms a coarse puree.

Form the hominy mixture into 6 cakes about 3 inches in diameter. Place the cakes in a greased baking dish and top each with an equal portion of butter. Bake until lightly browned, about 20 minutes.

Makes 6 cakes

Surrullitos (Cheese Fritters)

2 cups water
½ teaspoon salt
1½ cups masa harina
1 cup shredded Cheddar, Edam, or Monterey Jack cheese
1 cup vegetable oil

Bring the water and salt to a rapid boil in a saucepan over high heat. Lower the heat to moderate and stir in the masa harina. Cook, stirring constantly with a wooden spoon, until the mixture thickens and begins to pull away from the sides of the saucepan, about 10 minutes. Remove the saucepan from the heat and stir in the cheese.

To make the fritters, form heaping teaspoonfuls of the dough into cigar shapes about ½ inch in diameter.

Fill a large, heavy skillet with the vegetable oil to a depth of 1 inch. Heat the oil over moderate-high heat until it is very hot and a small bit of the dough dropped into it sizzles immediately. Fry the surrullitos in the oil (in batches if necessary) until golden brown, about 3 to 5 minutes. Drain on paper towels and serve hot.

Makes about 20 fritters

Pueblo Lamb Stew

Juniper berries give this stew its Native American flavor. If you can't find the berries (try a gourmet shop) or don't like the distinctive flavor, just leave them out.

2 pounds boneless lamb, cubed
¼ cup flour
5 tablespoons vegetable oil
1 large onion, chopped
3 garlic cloves, finely chopped
2 cups canned or frozen hominy
2 large carrots, cut into thick slices
1 large turnip, peeled and diced
1 4-ounce can green chilies, seeded and chopped
5 cups chicken broth
1 teaspoon ground cumin
2 jalapeño peppers, seeded and diced
½ teaspoon dried oregano
6 dried juniper berries (optional)

Dredge the lamb cubes in the flour, shaking off any excess. Heat 2 tablespoons of the oil in a large skillet over moderate heat. Add the lamb cubes and cook until lightly browned all over, about 5 to 7 minutes. Set aside.

Heat the remaining oil in a large, 4-quart pot over moderate heat. Add the onions and garlic and cook, stirring often, until the onion softens, about 5 minutes. Add the reserved lamb along with the hominy, carrots, turnip, green chilies, chicken broth, cumin, jalapeños, oregano, and juniper berries (if used). Bring the mixture to a boil, then reduce the heat to low and cover the pot. Simmer, stirring occasionally, until the lamb and hominy are tender, about 45 to 55 minutes.

Serves 4

Posole

Posole is a simple, traditional Southwestern dish made with hominy, pork, and red chilies. In Mexico, where this dish originated, it is spelled pozole; among Anglos, it is sometimes known less elegantly as hog and hominy. Whatever you call it, make it a day or two in advance for the best flavor. The longer you can simmer it, the better.

4 tablespoons bacon drippings or vegetable oil
1 large onion, coarsely chopped
4 garlic cloves, finely chopped
3 pounds boneless pork, cubed
4 cups canned or frozen hominy
2 tablespoons ground red chili powder
1 teaspoon ground cumin
1 teaspoon dried oregano
1 tablespoon salt
freshly ground black pepper to taste
4 cups chicken broth
water

Heat the bacon drippings in a large, 4-quart pot over moderate heat. Add the onion and garlic and cook, stirring often, until the onion is softened. Add the pork and cook, stirring often, until the pork is white on all sides.

Add the hominy, chili powder, cumin, oregano, salt, black pepper, and chicken broth. Add enough water to cover all the ingredients to a depth of 3 inches. Bring the mixture to a boil and skim off any scum. Reduce the heat to very low and simmer, stirring occasionally, until the hominy and pork are very tender, about 3 hours or longer. Add additional water as needed to keep the stew from drying out. Posole should be fairly soupy. Serve in bowls, accompanied by warm corn tortillas.

Serves 4

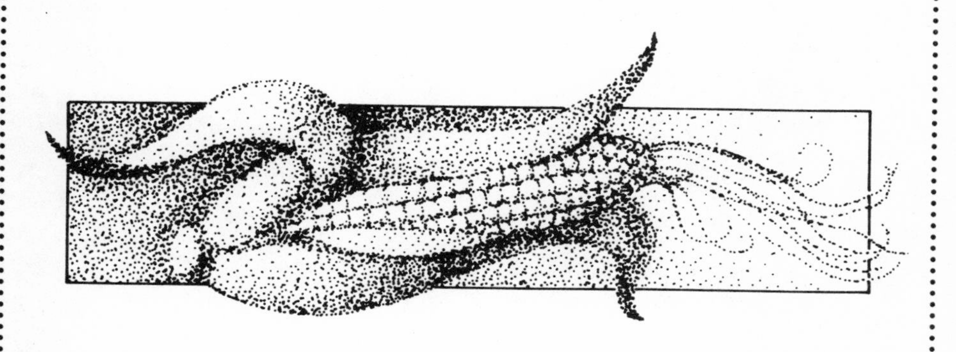

CHAPTER
8

Salads

Corn kernels in a salad add flavor, color, and texture. As always, fresh kernels cut from the cob are best, but these salads are also quite good when made with canned or frozen kernels. Corn salads range from simple side dishes to substantial combinations that can easily serve as main-course dishes. Most can be prepared ahead of time—indeed, many benefit from standing before being served—making corn salads particularly good for summer meals and buffet entertaining.

Corn Salad with Peppers

2 cups corn kernels
2 green bell peppers, seeded and coarsely diced
1/2 cup chopped red onion
1/3 cup red wine vinegar
2 teaspoons ground cumin
salt to taste
freshly ground black pepper to taste

Combine all ingredients in a serving bowl and toss gently. Chill thoroughly before serving.

Serves 4

Warm Corn Salad with Peppers

3 tablespoons extra-virgin olive oil
3 large shallots, coarsely chopped
1 red bell pepper, seeded and cut into strips
1 yellow bell pepper, seeded and cut into strips
salt to taste
freshly ground black pepper to taste
3 cups corn kernels
1 large garlic clove, finely chopped
1/4 teaspoon dried thyme
1 tablespoon coarsely chopped fresh parsley
1 tablespoon balsamic vinegar

Heat the olive oil in a heavy skillet. Add the shallots and cook over low heat, stirring often, until the shallots are softened. Add the red and yellow pepper strips and salt and pepper to taste. Cook, stirring occasionally, until the peppers are softened, about 10 minutes.

Using a slotted spoon, remove the peppers and shallots from the skillet and reserve them in a serving bowl.

Add the corn kernels and garlic to the skillet and cook, stirring occasionally, until the corn is heated through, about 5 minutes. Using a slotted spoon, add the corn and garlic to the reserved peppers.

Add the thyme, parsley, vinegar and additional black pepper and toss gently. Serve warm.

Serves 4

Charred Corn and Tomato Salad

When making this salad for a barbecue, be sure to put the corn on to grill first.

4 ears fresh corn, husked
4 tablespoons extra-virgin olive oil
2 tablespoons cider vinegar
2 tablespoons Dijon mustard
2 garlic cloves, finely chopped
½ teaspoon ground cumin
1 teaspoon salt
freshly ground black pepper to taste
4 large, ripe tomatoes, seeded and coarsely chopped
4 tablespoons chopped red onion
2 tablespoons finely chopped fresh coriander

Preheat the broiler to high or prepare a hot charcoal or gas grill.

Grill the corn ears, turning occasionally, until the kernels begin to char, about 10 to 15 minutes. Do not let the ears burn. Remove the ears and let cool.

Cut the kernels from the cobs with a sharp knife. Set the kernels aside.

Make the dressing by combining the olive oil, vinegar, mustard, garlic, cumin, salt, and black pepper in a mixing bowl. Whisk well.

Put the corn kernels, chopped tomatoes, red onion, and coriander in a serving bowl. Pour the dressing over the mixture and toss well.

Serves 4

Italian Corn Salad

2 cups corn kernels
3 large, ripe tomatoes, seeded and diced
¼ pound mozzarella cheese, cubed
⅓ cup coarsely chopped fresh basil leaves
5 tablespoons extra-virgin olive oil
2 tablespoons balsamic vinegar
salt to taste
freshly ground black pepper to taste

Combine the corn kernels, tomatoes, mozzarella, and basil in a serving bowl. In a small bowl, whisk together the olive oil, vinegar, and salt and pepper to taste. Pour the dressing over the salad and toss gently. Let stand 20 minutes before serving.

Serves 4

Corn and Black Bean Salad

1 cup corn kernels
1 cup cooked black beans
2 large, ripe tomatoes, seeded and coarsely diced
1 small onion, finely diced
2 jalapeño peppers, seeded and finely diced
⅓ cup coarsely chopped cilantro leaves
2 tablespoons lime juice
2 tablespoons extra-virgin olive oil
1½ teaspoons salt
freshly ground black pepper to taste

Combine all ingredients in a serving bowl. Stir gently and let stand for 30 minutes before serving.

Serves 4

Corn and Lentil Salad

1 cup cooked brown lentils, drained
1 cup corn kernels
1 celery stalk, coarsely chopped
¼ cup chopped pimento
1 scallion, thinly sliced
3 tablespoons extra-virgin olive oil
1 tablespoon balsamic vinegar
1 large garlic clove, finely chopped
½ teaspoon ground cumin
salt to taste

Combine the lentils, corn, celery, pimento, and scallion in a serving bowl.

In a small bowl, whisk together the olive oil, vinegar, garlic, cumin, and salt to taste.

Pour the dressing over the salad and toss gently. Serve at room temperature.

Serves 4

Marinated Chickpea Salad with Corn

1 cup cooked chickpeas
1 cup corn kernels
¼ cup chopped red onion
1 large carrot, shredded
1 celery stalk, finely chopped
3 tablespoons extra-virgin olive oil
1 tablespoon cider vinegar
1 large garlic clove, finely chopped
½ teaspoon dry mustard

½ teaspoon paprika
salt to taste
freshly ground black pepper to taste

Combine the chickpeas, corn, onion, carrot, and celery in a serving bowl.

In a small bowl, whisk together the olive oil, vinegar, garlic, dry mustard, paprika, and salt and pepper to taste.

Pour the dressing over the salad and toss gently. Let stand 2 hours at room temperature before serving.

Serves 4

Avocado Corn Salad

1½ cups corn kernels
½ cup thinly sliced red onion
1 ripe avocado, peeled and cut into small cubes
2 jalapeño peppers, seeded and finely chopped
½ cup coarsely chopped cilantro leaves
3 tablespoons extra-virgin olive oil
1 tablespoon balsamic vinegar
salt to taste
freshly ground black pepper to taste

Combine the corn kernels, red onion, avocado, jalapeños, and cilantro leaves in a serving bowl.

In a small bowl whisk together the olive oil, vinegar, and salt and pepper to taste.

Pour the dressing over the salad, toss very gently, and let stand at room temperature for 3 hours before serving.

Serves 4

Corn Salad with Mayonnaise Dressing

For a Southwestern version of this salad, omit the basil leaves and mix in 1 teaspoon chili powder with the mayonnaise.

2 cups corn kernels
1/2 cup diced red bell pepper
1/2 cup chopped fresh basil leaves
1/4 cup chopped scallion
1/4 cup sliced green olives
1 cup mayonnaise
salt to taste
freshly ground black pepper to taste

Combine the corn kernels, red pepper, basil, scallion, and olives in a serving bowl. Stir in the mayonnaise and season to taste with salt and pepper.

Serves 4

Corn and Smoked Sausage Salad

3 tablespoons vegetable oil
1 1/2 pounds smoked sausage or kielbasa, thinly sliced
1 1/2 cups corn kernels
1 green bell pepper, seeded and coarsely diced
3 scallions, thinly sliced
10 romaine lettuce leaves, torn into bite-sized pieces
3 tablespoons red wine vinegar
2 tablespoons brown sugar
2 tablespoons coarse mustard

$^2/_3$ cup extra-virgin olive oil
freshly ground black pepper to taste

Heat the vegetable oil in a heavy skillet over medium heat. Add the sausage slices and cook until lightly browned on both sides, about 8 minutes. Drain well.

Combine the sausage, corn, green pepper, scallions, and lettuce pieces in a large serving bowl.

In a small bowl, whisk together the vinegar, brown sugar, and mustard. Whisk in the olive oil. Add black pepper to taste.

Pour the dressing over the salad and toss gently. Serve at once.

Serves 4

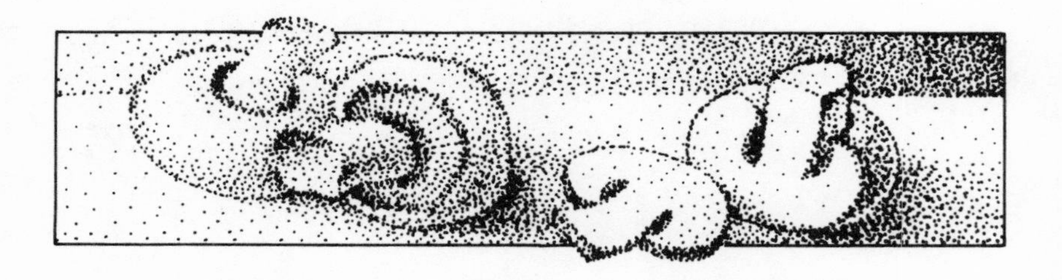

Corn and Chicken Salad with Herb Dressing

2 cups corn kernels
$1\frac{1}{2}$ cups cubed cooked chicken
1 small zucchini, thinly sliced
1 ripe tomato, seeded and thinly sliced
1 green bell pepper, seeded and thinly sliced
$^1/_4$ cup thinly sliced red onion
1 large garlic clove, finely chopped
3 tablespoons extra-virgin olive oil
2 tablespoons red wine vinegar

½ teaspoon salt
2 tablespoons chopped fresh parsley
1 tablespoon chopped fresh basil, or ½ teaspoon dried basil
¼ teaspoon chopped fresh thyme, or ⅛ teaspoon dried thyme
¼ teaspoon ground cumin

Combine the corn, chicken, zucchini, tomato, green pepper, and red onion in a serving bowl.

In small bowl, whisk together the garlic, olive oil, vinegar, salt, parsley, basil, thyme, and cumin.

Pour the dressing over the salad and toss gently. Serve at room temperature.

Serves 4

Southwestern Chicken Corn Salad

This salad is excellent served warm; it's also a good way to use up left-overs from a barbecue.

4 grilled, boneless chicken breasts, cubed
1½ cups grilled corn kernels (see Chapter 1)
½ cup diced roasted red bell pepper
3 scallions, thinly sliced
1 tablespoon chopped fresh cilantro
1 jalapeño pepper, seeded and finely chopped
1 tablespoon extra-virgin olive oil
1 teaspoon lime juice
½ teaspoon salt
freshly ground black pepper to taste

Combine the chicken, corn kernels, roasted red pepper, and scallions in a serving bowl. In a small bowl, whisk together the cilantro, jalapeño pepper, olive oil, lime juice, salt, and black pepper to taste.

Pour the dressing over the salad, toss lightly, and serve at once.

Serves 4

Corn, Lima, and Ham Salad

What's the definition of eternity? Two people and a large ham. Try this salad to use up leftover ham. If you can't stand lima beans, try substituting cooked fresh peas.

2 cups cooked lima beans
1 cup corn kernels
1 cup diced cooked ham
3 tablespoons extra-virgin olive oil
2 tablespoons lemon juice
2 teaspoons chopped fresh dill or 1/2 teaspoon dried dill
salt to taste
freshly ground black pepper to taste

Combine the lima beans, corn kernels, and ham in a serving bowl.

In a small bowl, whisk together the olive oil, lemon juice, dill, and salt and pepper to taste.

Pour the dressing over the salad and toss gently. Chill well and serve cold.

Serves 4

Baby Corn Salad

Baby corn is sometimes hard to find in the supermarket. Check the Oriental foods section.

1 1-pound can baby corn
1 red bell pepper, seeded and cut into strips
1 green bell pepper, seeded and cut into strips
1 large garlic clove, finely chopped

4 tablespoons peanut oil
2 tablespoons rice vinegar
1 teaspoon sesame oil
several drops hot chili oil
2 tablespoons chopped cilantro leaves

Drain the baby corn and rinse well in cold water. Drain thoroughly again.

Combine the baby corn, red pepper, and green pepper in a serving bowl.

In a small bowl, whisk together the garlic, peanut oil, rice vinegar, sesame oil, and hot chili oil.

Pour the dressing over the salad and toss well. Let stand at room temperature 1 to 2 hours. Add the cilantro and toss again before serving.

CHAPTER
9

Cornbread

The earliest colonists in the New World learned to make simple, unleavened cornbreads—just cornmeal, salt, and water—from the Native Americans. *These breads were cooked over open fires, not baked (stoves didn't become part of the American kitchen until much later), and go by a confusing variety of names.* *The oldest may be pone, which is probably derived from the Native American word* apan, *describing a very simple, unleavened cornmeal cake baked in ashes.*

Thus, corn pones are sometimes called ashcakes. ✂ They are also called hoecakes, because early settlers supposedly baked them on the blades of hoes. ✂ Yet another name for these flat breads is johnnycakes. ✂ This name may derive from "journeycake," meaning a bread taken on a trip, or possibly from Shawnee cake, referring to that Native American nation, or possibly from some other source.

Baked cornbread using chemical leavens was first developed when baking soda was introduced to the American housewife in the 1850s. ✂ Baking powder came along in the late 1860s. ✂ Combining leavens with cornmeal and some wheat flour allowed moister, less crumbly cornbreads to be made—and the batter could also be used for muffins. ✂ Finally, commercial yeast, also a product of the 1860s, made raised breads combining cornmeal and wheat flour easier to make.

Cornmeal comes in both yellow and white. ✂ There is absolutely no difference in quality or flavor between the two. In the recipes below, yellow cornmeal is sometimes specified strictly for its appearance. ✂ There is one difference among cornmeals, however. ✂ Stone-ground cornmeals are definitely preferred, because they retain more of the corn germ and oil and thus more of the rich corny flavor. ✂ If your food market doesn't carry stone-ground cornmeal, check your local health-food store.

Cornbread can be made in a standard baking dish, but the optimal method is to use a well-seasoned, 9- or 10-inch cast-iron skillet. ✂ When you turn on the oven to preheat it, place the recipe's butter or bacon drippings in the skillet and put it in the oven. ✂

By the time you are ready for it, the shortening will be melted and the skillet will be very hot. Swirl the shortening around to coat the skillet and then pour it into the batter. Immediately stir and pour the batter back into the hot skillet—you will hear a very satisfying sizzle. Bake as usual. The cornbread will have a wonderfully crispy brown bottom crust.

In this chapter, only baked cornbreads containing a leavening agent are discussed. Recipes for flat and stove-top cornbreads and other variations are found in Chapter 10.

AUTHENTIC CORNBREAD

Most Southerners would agree that this recipe is the genuine article, since it uses very little flour and no sugar. Yankee cornbread contains sugar, but Southerners consider that cake. You must use bacon drippings and make it in a 9-inch cast-iron skillet.

2 tablespoons bacon drippings
1½ cups cornmeal
3 tablespoons flour
1½ teaspoons baking powder
½ teaspoon salt
1 egg
1½ cups milk

Preheat the oven to 450°. Place the drippings in the skillet and place the skillet in the oven while preparing the batter.

In a mixing bowl, combine the cornmeal, flour, baking powder, and salt.

In another mixing bowl, beat together the egg and milk. Pour the mixture into the dry ingredients and stir until they are just mixed.

Remove the skillet from the oven. Swirl the melted bacon drippings around to coat the skillet bottom and sides. Pour the remaining drippings into the batter. Stir briefly, then immediately pour the batter back into the hot skillet. Bake until the cornbread is golden brown and begins to pull away from the sides of the skillet, about 20 minutes.

Serves 4 to 6

Cornbread

This fundamental recipe for a slightly sweet, moist cornbread is an excellent base for creative cooking. Try adding a cup of fresh blueberries, a cup of shredded cheese, a few slices of crumbled bacon, a teaspoon or two of dried herbs such as parsley or dill, or (of course) a cup of corn kernels.

1 cup cornmeal
1 cup flour
¼ cup sugar
1 tablespoon baking powder
½ teaspoon salt
2 eggs
4 tablespoons unsalted butter, melted
1 cup milk

Preheat the oven to 400°.

Combine the cornmeal, flour, sugar, baking powder, and salt in a mixing bowl. Mix well.

In another mixing bowl, beat together the eggs, butter, and milk. Pour the mixture into the dry ingredients and stir until they are just mixed.

Pour the batter into a greased 8-inch baking pan or heavy cast-iron skillet. Bake until the cornbread is golden brown and pulls away from the sides of the pan, about 20 to 25 minutes.

Serves 4 to 6

EXTRA-RICH CORNBREAD

1½ cups cornmeal
½ cup flour
2 tablespoons sugar
3 teaspoons baking powder
½ teaspoon salt
3 eggs
6 tablespoons unsalted butter, melted
1 cup milk
¼ cup heavy cream

Preheat the oven to 400°.

Combine the cornmeal, flour, sugar, baking powder, and salt in a mixing bowl. Mix well.

In another mixing bowl, beat together the eggs, butter, milk, and cream. Pour the mixture into the dry ingredients and stir until they are just mixed.

Pour the batter into a greased 8-inch baking pan or cast-iron skillet. Bake until the cornbread is golden brown and pulls away from the sides of the pan, about 20 to 25 minutes.

Serves 4 to 6

BUTTERMILK CORNBREAD

If you don't have buttermilk on hand, substitute an equal amount of milk mixed with ½ teaspoon white vinegar or 1 tablespoon lemon juice. Or just use plain milk—the cornbread will taste fine but be slightly less crispy.

2 cups cornmeal
1 teaspoon baking powder
½ teaspoon baking soda
½ teaspoon salt

2 eggs

2 tablespoons unsalted butter, melted

1½ cups buttermilk

Preheat the oven to 450°.

Combine the cornmeal, baking powder, baking soda, and salt in a mixing bowl. Mix well.

In another mixing bowl, beat together the eggs, butter, and buttermilk. Pour the mixture into the dry ingredients and stir until they are just mixed.

Pour the batter into a greased 8-inch baking pan or heavy cast-iron skillet. Bake until the cornbread is golden brown and pulls away from the sides of the pan, about 20 to 25 minutes.

Serves 4 to 6

Whole Wheat Cornbread

1 cup cornmeal

½ cup whole wheat flour

1 tablespoon baking powder

½ teaspoon baking soda

1/4 teaspoon salt

2 eggs

1 cup plain, low-fat yogurt

1½ tablespoons unsalted butter, melted

1½ tablespoons corn oil

½ cup milk

1 tablespoon honey

Preheat the oven to 425°.

Combine the cornmeal, whole wheat flour, baking powder, baking soda, and salt in a mixing bowl. Mix well.

In another mixing bowl, beat together the eggs, yogurt, butter, corn oil, milk, and honey. Mix well. Pour the mixture into the dry ingredients and stir until they are just mixed.

Pour the batter into a greased 8-inch baking pan or heavy cast-iron skillet. Bake until the cornbread is golden brown and the edges pull away from the sides of the pan, about 20 to 25 minutes.

Serves 4 to 6

DROWNED CORNBREAD

This is an old Southern favorite, a cross between cornbread and spoonbread. Use yellow cornmeal for an attractive appearance. This is one cornbread recipe where the buttermilk is a must.

1 1/2 cups cornmeal
1/2 cup flour
1/2 cup sugar
1 teaspoon baking soda
1/2 teaspoon salt
2 eggs
3 tablespoons unsalted butter, melted
1 cup buttermilk
1 cup light cream or half-and-half

Preheat the oven to 400°.

Combine the cornmeal, flour, sugar, baking soda, and salt in a mixing bowl. Mix well.

In another mixing bowl, beat together the eggs, butter, and buttermilk. Pour the mixture into the dry ingredients and stir until they are just mixed.

Pour the batter into a greased 8-inch baking pan or heavy cast-iron skillet. Pour the cream over the surface—do not stir. Bake until the cornbread has rich yellow custard on top and the edges pull away from the sides of the pan, about 25 to 30 minutes.

Serves 4 to 6

Maple Cornbread

1 1/2 cups cornmeal

1/2 cup flour

1 tablespoon baking powder

1/2 teaspoon baking soda

1/2 teaspoon salt

1 egg

1 1/2 cups buttermilk

3 tablespoons unsalted butter, melted

4 tablespoons pure maple syrup

Preheat the oven to 425°.

Combine the cornmeal, flour, baking powder, baking soda, and salt in a mixing bowl. Mix well.

In another mixing bowl, beat together the egg, buttermilk, butter, and maple syrup. Pour the mixture into the dry ingredients and stir until they are just mixed.

Pour the batter into a greased 8-inch baking pan or cast-iron skillet. Bake until the cornbread is golden brown and pulls away from the sides of the pan, about 20 minutes.

Serves 4 to 6

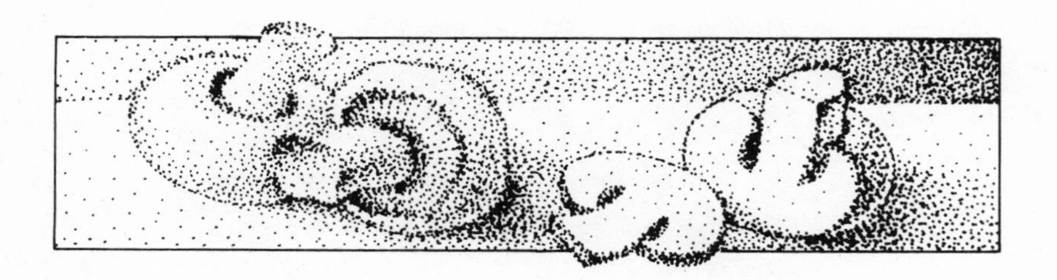

Applesauce Cornbread

This is an excellent breakfast bread.

1 cup cornmeal
2 cups whole wheat flour
1 teaspoon baking soda
3/4 teaspoon salt
1 cup buttermilk
2/3 cup honey
3/4 cup unsweetened applesauce
1 cup golden raisins

Preheat the oven to 350°.

Combine the cornmeal, whole wheat flour, baking soda, and salt in a mixing bowl. Mix well.

In another mixing bowl, beat together the buttermilk and honey. Pour the mixture into the dry ingredients and stir until they are just mixed. Add the applesauce and raisins and stir until they are just evenly mixed.

Pour the batter into a greased 8-inch baking pan or cast-iron skillet. Bake until the cornbread is golden brown and pulls away from the sides of the pan, about 40 minutes.

Serves 4 to 6

Apple Upside-Down Cornbread

Great for brunch.

6 tablespoons pure maple syrup
8 tablespoons (1 stick) unsalted butter, melted
2 large tart apples, peeled, cored, and thinly sliced
1 1/2 cups cornmeal

1/2 cup flour
2 tablespoons sugar
3 teaspoons baking powder
1/2 teaspoon salt
3 eggs
1 cup milk
1/4 cup heavy cream

Preheat the oven to 375°.

In a cast-iron or ovenproof skillet, heat 2 tablespoons of the maple syrup with 2 tablespoons of the butter over medium heat. Add the apples and sauté until softened, about 5 minutes. Arrange the apple slices evenly in the skillet and remove from the heat.

Combine the cornmeal, flour, sugar, baking powder, and salt in a mixing bowl. Mix well.

In another mixing bowl, beat together the remaining maple syrup and butter, eggs, milk, and cream. Pour the mixture into the dry ingredients and stir until they are just mixed.

Spread the cornmeal batter evenly over the apple slices. Bake for 30 to 35 minutes, or until a toothpick inserted into the center comes out clean. Remove from the oven and let cool in the skillet for 5 minutes. Invert the skillet onto a 12-inch or larger serving platter and cut the cornbread into wedges. Serve at once with additional maple syrup.

Serves 4 to 6

Spinach Cornbread

2 tablespoons unsalted butter
1 shallot, finely chopped
4 cups coarsely chopped fresh spinach, well rinsed
1 1/2 cups cornmeal
1/2 cup flour
2 teaspoons baking soda

1/2 teaspoon baking powder

1/2 teaspoon salt

1/4 teaspoon ground nutmeg

freshly ground black pepper to taste

1 egg

1 cup milk

1/2 cup sour cream

Preheat the oven to 425°.

Melt the butter in a skillet over moderate heat. Add the shallot and cook, stirring often, until softened, about 1 minute. Add the spinach, cover, and cook, stirring occasionally, until the spinach is thoroughly wilted, about 7 to 10 minutes. Uncover and raise the heat. Continue to cook, stirring often, until most of the liquid has evaporated, about 1 to 2 minutes longer. Set aside.

Combine the cornmeal, flour, baking soda, baking powder, salt, nutmeg, and lots of black pepper in a mixing bowl. Mix well.

Stir in the egg, milk, and sour cream. Mix well. Stir in the reserved spinach mixture.

Pour the batter into a greased 8-inch baking pan or cast-iron skillet. Bake until the cornbread is golden brown and pulls away from the sides of the pan, about 15 to 20 minutes.

Serves 4 to 6

PUMPKIN CORNBREAD

1 cup yellow cornmeal

1 cup flour

3 tablespoons sugar

1 tablespoon baking powder

1 teaspoon baking soda

1/2 teaspoon salt

1/4 teaspoon ground ginger

1/4 teaspoon ground cinnamon

1/4 teaspoon ground nutmeg
2 eggs
1 cup sour cream
1 cup pureed pumpkin (canned or fresh)
8 tablespoons unsalted butter, melted
1/2 cup golden raisins
1/2 cup coarsely chopped pecans

Preheat the oven to 425°.

Combine the cornmeal, flour, sugar, baking powder, baking soda, salt, ground ginger, ground cinnamon, and ground nutmeg in a mixing bowl. Mix well.

In another mixing bowl, beat together the eggs, sour cream, pumpkin, and butter. Pour the mixture into the dry ingredients and stir until they are just mixed. Add the raisins and pecans and stir until they are just mixed in.

Pour the batter into a greased 8-inch baking pan or cast-iron skillet. Bake until the cornbread is golden brown and pulls away from the sides of the pan, about 20 to 25 minutes.

Serve warm.

Serves 4 to 6

Jalapeño Cornbread

1/4 cup sun-dried tomatoes
2 cups cornmeal
1 tablespoon sugar
2 teaspoons baking soda
1 teaspoon salt
1 teaspoon ground red chili powder
2 eggs
3 tablespoons bacon drippings
1 cup buttermilk
2 scallions, finely chopped

1/4 cup finely chopped mild green chilies
2 jalapeño peppers, seeded and finely chopped

Place the sun-dried tomatoes in a small bowl and add enough boiling water to cover. Soak until softened, about 10 minutes. Drain and chop. Set aside.

Preheat the oven to 350°.

Combine the cornmeal, sugar, baking soda, salt, and chili powder in a mixing bowl. Mix well.

In another mixing bowl, beat together the eggs, bacon drippings, and buttermilk. Pour the mixture into the dry ingredients and stir until they are just mixed. Add the scallions, green chilies, jalapeño peppers, and reserved sun-dried tomatoes and stir until they are just mixed in.

Pour the batter into a greased 8-inch baking pan or cast-iron skillet. Bake until the cornbread is golden brown and pulls away from the sides of the pan, about 25 to 30 minutes.

Serves 4 to 6

Corn Muffins

Many variations of this basic recipe are possible, but additions that make it sweeter—such as a cup of fresh blueberries and a pinch of cinnamon—seem to work best.

1 cup cornmeal
1 cup flour
1/4 cup sugar
3 teaspoons baking powder
1/2 teaspoon salt
1 egg
1 cup milk
5 tablespoons unsalted butter, melted

Preheat the oven to 375°. Lightly grease a muffin tin or tins.

Combine the cornmeal, flour, sugar, baking powder, and salt in a mixing bowl. Mix well.

In another mixing bowl, beat together the egg, milk, and melted butter. Pour the mixture into the dry ingredients and stir until they are just mixed. Do not overmix.

Spoon enough batter into the cups of the muffin tin to fill them two-thirds full. Bake until the muffins are golden brown, about 12 to 15 minutes.

Makes about 8 muffins

HUSHPUPPY MUFFINS

1 cup cornmeal
1 teaspoon salt
1/2 teaspoon sugar
1/4 teaspoon cayenne pepper
1/8 teaspoon ground thyme
2 scallions, finely chopped
1 cup boiling water
1 egg, beaten
1 tablespoon bacon drippings or unsalted butter, melted
1 teaspoon hot sauce

Preheat the oven to 450°. Lightly grease a muffin tin with small cups.

In a mixing bowl, combine the cornmeal, salt, sugar, cayenne pepper, thyme, and scallions. Stir well.

Make a well in the center and pour in the boiling water. Stir well. Stir in the egg, bacon drippings, and hot sauce. Do not overmix.

Spoon enough batter into the cups of the muffin tin to fill them two-thirds full. Bake until the muffins are golden brown, about 12 to 15 minutes.

Makes about 12 small muffins

Sweet Red Pepper Muffins

2 tablespoons unsalted butter
1 medium red bell pepper, seeded and finely chopped
1 1/4 cups cornmeal
1 cup flour
1/4 cup brown sugar
1 1/2 teaspoons baking soda
1/2 teaspoon baking powder
1/2 teaspoon salt
1 egg
1 cup plain low-fat yogurt

Preheat the oven to 400°. Lightly grease a muffin tin or tins.

Melt the butter in a small skillet over moderate heat. Add the red pepper and cook, stirring often, until the pepper is softened, about 8 minutes. Set aside.

In a mixing bowl, combine the cornmeal, flour, brown sugar, baking soda, baking powder, and salt. Stir well.

In another bowl, beat the egg with the yogurt. Add the reserved red pepper and any liquid from the skillet and mix well. Pour the mixture into the dry ingredients and stir until they are just mixed. Do not overmix.

Spoon enough batter into the cups of the muffin tin to fill them two-thirds full. Bake until the muffins are golden brown, about 15 to 20 minutes. Do not remove muffins from the tin until they are somewhat cooled, about 10 minutes.

Makes about 12 muffins

Molasses Muffins

1 cup cornmeal
1 cup white flour
1 tablespoon baking powder
1 teaspoon baking soda

½ teaspoon salt
4 tablespoons melted sweet butter
½ cup dark unsulphured molasses
1 cup buttermilk
1 egg

Preheat the oven to 400°. Grease a muffin tin or tins.

Combine the cornmeal, flour, baking powder, baking soda, and salt in a large mixing bowl.

In another bowl, combine the melted butter and molasses. Stir until well mixed.

In another bowl, whisk together the buttermilk and egg. Add the butter and molasses mixture and whisk until combined.

Add the liquid ingredients to the dry and mix until just combined. Do not overmix.

Half-fill the cups of the greased muffin tin with the mixture and bake for 12 to 15 minutes or until lightly browned.

Makes 12 muffins

Sour Cream Corn Muffins

1 cup cornmeal
1 cup flour
¼ cup sugar
2 teaspoons baking powder
½ teaspoon baking soda
1 teaspoon salt
2 eggs
1 cup sour cream
4 tablespoons unsalted butter, melted

Preheat the oven to 425°. Lightly grease two 12-muffin tins with small cups.

Combine the cornmeal, flour, sugar, baking powder, baking soda, and salt in a mixing bowl. Mix well.

In another mixing bowl, beat together the eggs, sour cream, and butter. Pour the mixture into the dry ingredients and stir until they are just mixed. Do not overmix.

Spoon enough batter into the cups of the muffin tin to fill them two-thirds full. Bake until the muffins are golden brown, about 10 to 12 minutes. Serve warm.

Makes about 24 small muffins

Extra-Corny Muffins

1 cup yellow cornmeal
1 cup flour
½ cup brown sugar
2 teaspoons baking soda
½ teaspoon salt
1 egg
2 tablespoons unsalted butter, melted
1 17-ounce can cream-style corn

Preheat the oven to 350°. Lightly grease a muffin tin or tins.

In a mixing bowl, combine the cornmeal, flour, brown sugar, baking soda, and salt. Stir well.

In another bowl, beat the egg with the butter and cream-style corn. Pour the mixture into the dry ingredients and stir until they are just mixed. Do not overmix.

Spoon enough batter into the cups of the muffin tin to fill them two-thirds full. Bake until the muffins are golden brown, about 15 to 20 minutes.

Makes about 12 muffins

Pecan Corn Muffins

$1\frac{1}{2}$ cups cornmeal
1 cup flour
4 teaspoons baking powder
½ teaspoon salt
1 egg
4 tablespoons unsalted butter, melted
1 cup milk
½ cup honey
1 cup finely chopped pecans

Preheat the oven to 400°. Lightly grease a muffin tin or tins.

Combine the cornmeal, flour, sugar, baking powder, and salt in a mixing bowl. Mix well.

In another mixing bowl, beat together the egg, butter, milk, and honey. Pour the mixture into the dry ingredients and stir until they are just mixed. Add the chopped pecans and stir again. Do not overmix.

Spoon enough batter into the cups of the muffin tin to fill them two-thirds full. Bake until the muffins are golden brown, about 15 to 20 minutes.

Makes about 12 muffins

Orange Corn Muffins

⅓ cup orange marmalade
1 cup yellow cornmeal
1 cup flour
3 teaspoons baking powder
½ teaspoon salt
2 eggs

4 tablespoons unsalted butter, melted
3/4 cup milk

Preheat the oven to 425°. Lightly grease a muffin tin or tins.

In a small saucepan over low heat, melt the marmalade. Set aside.

Combine the cornmeal, flour, baking powder, and salt in a mixing bowl. Mix well.

In another mixing bowl, beat together the eggs, butter, milk, and reserved marmalade. Pour the mixture into the dry ingredients and stir until they are just mixed. Do not overmix.

Spoon enough batter into the cups of the muffin tin to fill them two-thirds full. Bake until the muffins are golden brown, about 15 to 20 minutes.

Makes about 12 muffins

RASPBERRY CORN MUFFINS

1 cup yellow cornmeal
1 cup flour
1/2 cup brown sugar
1 teaspoon baking powder
1/2 teaspoon baking soda
1/2 teaspoon salt
1 egg
4 tablespoons unsalted butter, melted
1/2 cup plain low-fat yogurt
1/2 cup orange juice
1 teaspoon grated orange rind
1 cup raspberries

Preheat the oven to 400°. Lightly grease a muffin tin or tins.

Combine the cornmeal, flour, brown sugar, baking powder, baking soda, and salt in a mixing bowl. Mix well.

In another mixing bowl, beat together the egg, butter, yogurt, and orange juice. Pour the mixture into the dry ingredients and stir until they are just mixed. Add the orange rind and raspberries and mix again. Do not overmix.

Spoon enough batter into the cups of the muffin tin to fill them two-thirds full. Bake until the muffins are golden brown, about 12 to 15 minutes. Do not remove muffins from the tin until they are somewhat cooled, about 10 minutes.

Makes about 12 muffins

Corn Zephyrs

½ cup white cornmeal
½ teaspoon salt
1 tablespoon unsalted butter
1 cup boiling water
2 eggs, separated

Preheat the oven to 400°. Lightly grease a baking sheet.

In a heavy, 2-quart saucepan, combine the cornmeal, salt, and butter. Turn the heat to low and immediately pour in the boiling water. Cook, stirring constantly, until the mixture thickens, about 5 minutes. Remove from the heat and set aside.

In a small bowl, beat the egg whites until they are stiff but not dry.

Stir the egg yolks into the reserved cornmeal mixture. Fold in the egg whites.

Drop the batter by teaspoonfuls onto the baking sheet. Bake until the zephyrs are puffed and lightly browned, about 20 minutes. Serve hot.

Makes about 20

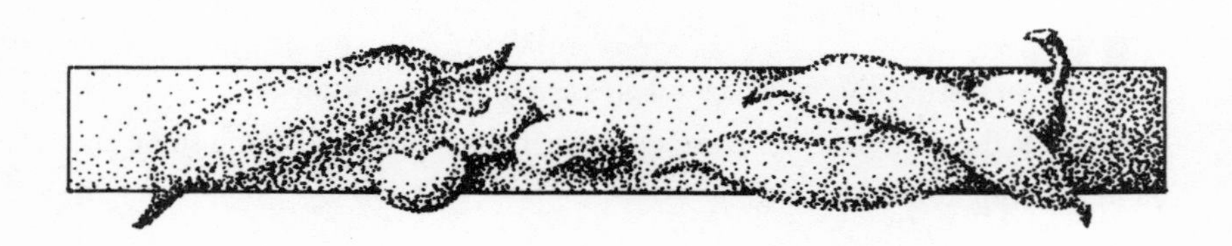

CORNMEAL DUMPLINGS

Serve these light dumplings in any soup or stew.

¾ cup white flour
¼ cup yellow cornmeal
¼ teaspoon salt
1¼ teaspoons baking powder
1 tablespoon cold unsalted butter, cut into small pieces
⅓ cup milk
freshly gound black pepper to taste
3 cups chicken or other broth

Combine the flour, cornmeal, salt, and baking powder in a mixing bowl. Using a pastry blender, two knives, or your fingers, cut in the butter until the mixture resembles coarse crumbs.

Add the milk and black pepper and stir until just mixed. Do not overmix.

Roll the dumpling dough out on a floured surface until it is 1/4 inch thick. Using a sharp knife, cut the dough into 1-inch squares.

To cook the dumplings, bring the broth to a simmer in a large pot with a tightly fitting lid. Drop in the dumplings, cover the pot tightly, and simmer until the dumplings are puffed, about 20 minutes.

Makes about 20 dumplings

CORN ROTI

This simple bread from India has a rich, corny flavor.

2 cups corn kernels
⅓ teaspoon salt
1¼ cups white flour, plus additional flour for rolling
1 tablespoon vegetable oil

Puree the corn kernels and salt in a food processor or blender. Pour the mixture into a medium mixing bowl. Mix in the flour 1/4 cup at a time, using a wooden spoon or your hands, until a soft, somewhat sticky dough is formed. Coat the dough with the vegetable oil.

Divide the dough into 12 equal portions. Roll each portion into a ball, then roll each ball out into a 6-inch round. Dust often with additional flour to prevent sticking. Cover each round with a clean kitchen towel; do not let the rounds touch one another.

Heat a cast-iron skillet or heavy frying pan over high heat for 3 minutes. Lower the heat to medium and place a round in the skillet. Cook until the underside is spotted with brown, about 1 1/2 minutes. Turn the round over and cook until the other side is spotted with brown, about 1 minute longer.

Keep the finished rounds warm in a low oven while cooking the rest. Serve at once.

Makes 12 breads

Buttermilk Scones

These scones are baked—a grave but delicious departure from tradition. An equal amount of candied fruit may be substituted for the raisins.

2 1/2 cups white flour
1 cup cornmeal
6 tablespoons sugar
2 1/2 tablespoons baking powder
1 teaspoon baking soda
1/4 teaspoon salt
10 tablespoons cold, unsalted butter, cut into small pieces
1 cup buttermilk
1 cup raisins

Preheat the oven to 350°. Lightly grease a baking sheet.

Combine the flour, cornmeal, sugar, baking powder, baking soda, and salt.

Using a pastry blender, two knives, or your fingers, cut in the butter until the mixture resembles coarse crumbs. Add the buttermilk in small amounts, stirring after each addition, until the mixture just combines to form a dough. (Use less or more buttermilk as needed.) Do not overmix.

Turn the dough out onto a lightly floured surface and knead in the raisins. Divide the dough in half. Lightly roll each portion into a circle about 1/2 inch thick. Cut each circle into wedge-shaped eighths.

Place the wedges on the lightly greased baking sheet and bake until browned on top, about 15 to 18 minutes.

Makes 16 scones

Cornmeal Biscuits

1 cup flour
1/2 cup cornmeal
1 1/2 teaspoons baking powder
1/2 teaspoon salt
6 tablespoons cold, unsalted butter, cut into small pieces
6 tablespoons milk

Preheat the oven to 425°. Line a baking sheet with aluminum foil.

Combine the flour, cornmeal, baking powder, and salt in a mixing bowl. Add the butter and mix, using a pastry blender or your fingers, until the mixture resembles coarse crumbs. Add the milk, stirring just until a soft dough is formed.

Turn the dough out onto a floured surface and pat it out to a thickness of about 1/2 inch. Use a biscuit cutter with a diameter of 1 1/2 inches to cut out the biscuits. Form the dough scraps into a sheet and cut out additional biscuits.

Place the biscuits on the baking sheet and bake until lightly browned on top, about 15 minutes (the biscuits will be darker brown on the bottom). Serve warm.

Makes about 16 biscuits

Sweet Potato Corn Pone

1 large sweet potato
8 tablespoons (1 stick) unsalted butter
4 eggs
½ cup brown sugar
1 teaspoon salt
1 teaspoon cinnamon
½ teaspoon baking soda
1 cup buttermilk
2 cups cornmeal
½ cup golden raisins
½ cup coarsely chopped pecans

Peel the sweet potato and cut it into small chunks. In a saucepan of boiling water, cook the chunks until very soft, about 25 minutes. Drain well. In a food processor or blender, puree the sweet potato. There should be about 2 cups.

Preheat the oven to 350°.

In a mixing bowl, combine the sweet potato puree with the butter. Mix well. Beat in the eggs, brown sugar, salt, cinnamon, and baking soda. Beat in the buttermilk. Stir in the cornmeal and mix well. Stir in the raisins and pecans.

Pour the batter into a greased 9-inch baking dish. Bake until browned on top, about 50 to 60 minutes.

Serves 4 to 6

Corn Pone with Pinto Beans

6 slices bacon, coarsely chopped
1 garlic clove, finely chopped
1 small onion, finely chopped
2 cups cooked pinto or kidney beans
1 teaspoon salt

1 teaspoon oregano

½ teaspoon hot red pepper flakes

freshly ground black pepper to taste

1 cup cornmeal

1 teaspoon baking soda

1 egg

2 tablespoons unsalted butter, melted

2 cups buttermilk

In a large, heavy skillet over moderate heat, cook the bacon pieces until they just begin to brown, about 4 minutes. Add the garlic and onion and cook, stirring often, until the onion is softened, about 5 minutes longer. Add the pinto beans, salt, oregano, red pepper flakes, and lots of black pepper. Stir well and reduce the heat to low. Continue to cook, stirring occasionally, while preparing the corn pone.

Combine the cornmeal, baking soda, and salt in a mixing bowl.

In another mixing bowl, beat together the egg, butter, and buttermilk. Pour the mixture into the dry ingredients and stir until they are just combined.

Spread the beans in the bottom of a greased 8-inch baking dish. Pour the cornmeal batter over the beans. Bake until the cornbread is golden brown and pulls away from the sides of the dish, about 25 to 30 minutes.

Serves 4

Corn and Rice Bread

1 cup cold cooked white rice

2 cups cornmeal

2½ teaspoons baking powder

1 teaspoon salt

3 eggs

2¼ cups milk

1 tablespoon unsalted butter, melted

Preheat the oven to 400°.

Push the rice through a coarse sieve. Set aside.

Combine the cornmeal, baking powder, and salt in a mixing bowl. Mix well.

In another mixing bowl, beat together the eggs and milk. Pour the mixture into the dry ingredients and mix well. Beat in the melted butter and reserved rice. Mix well.

Pour the batter into a greased 8-inch baking dish. Bake until golden brown, about 30 minutes. Serve hot.

Makes 1 loaf

PARAGUAYAN CORN BREAD

2 tablespoons unsalted butter
1 medium onion, finely chopped
3/4 cup corn kernels
3/4 cup yellow cornmeal
3/4 cup small-curd cottage cheese
3/4 cup shredded Muenster cheese
1/2 cup buttermilk
1/2 teaspoon salt
3 eggs, separated

Preheat the oven to 400°.

Melt the butter in a skillet over moderate heat. Add the onions and cook, stirring often, until softened, about 5 minutes. Set aside.

In a food processor or blender, puree the corn kernels. Pour the puree into a mixing bowl. Add the cornmeal, cottage cheese, Muenster cheese, buttermilk, salt, and reserved onions. Stir well.

In a small mixing bowl, beat the egg yolks until they are thick. In another mixing bowl, beat the egg whites until they form soft peaks. Gently fold the egg yolks into the whites. Fold the egg mixture into the cornmeal mixture.

Pour the batter into a greased 8-inch baking dish. Bake until browned on top, about 30 minutes. Serve warm.

Serves 4

Midwestern Supper Bread

2 tablespoons unsalted butter
1 medium onion, finely chopped
½ cup shredded Cheddar cheese
½ cup sour cream
1 cup yellow cornmeal
2 tablespoons flour
2 teaspoons baking powder
½ teaspoon salt
2 tablespoons sugar
1 egg
1 tablespoon corn oil
½ cup milk
1 4-ounce can green chili peppers, seeded and chopped
cayenne pepper to taste
freshly ground black pepper to taste

Melt the butter in a skillet over moderate heat. Add the onion and cook, stirring often, until softened, about 5 minutes. Set aside.

In a bowl, combine the cheese and sour cream. Set aside.

Combine the cornmeal, flour, baking powder, salt, and sugar in a mixing bowl. Mix well.

In another mixing bowl, beat together the egg, corn oil, and milk. Stir in the chopped chili peppers and season to taste with cayenne pepper and black pepper. Pour the mixture into the dry ingredients and stir until they are just mixed.

Pour the batter into a greased 8-inch loaf pan. Spread the reserved onion on top of the batter. Pour the reserved cheese and sour cream mixture over the onion. Bake until the top is golden and almost firm, about 30 minutes. Let cool in pan for 15 minutes before serving.

Serves 4 to 6

Tomato-Cheese Cornbread

1½ cups yellow cornmeal
½ cup flour
1 tablespoon baking powder
½ teaspoon baking soda
¼ teaspoon salt
3 eggs
¾ cup ricotta cheese
¾ cup tomato juice
3 tablespoons unsalted butter, melted
½ cup shredded Cheddar cheese
1 tablespoon grated Parmesan cheese

Preheat the oven to 425°.

Combine the cornmeal, flour, baking powder, baking soda, and salt in a mixing bowl. Mix well.

In another mixing bowl, beat the eggs with the ricotta cheese, tomato juice, and butter. Stir in the Cheddar cheese. Pour the mixture into the dry ingredients and stir until they are just mixed.

Pour the batter into a greased 8-inch baking dish. Sprinkle the Parmesan cheese evenly over the top. Bake until the cornbread is golden brown and pulls away from the edges of the dish, about 20 minutes. Serve warm.

Serves 4

Navajo Kneel-Down Bread

Many Native American breads are made by wrapping corn kernels or cornmeal in corn husks and then steaming or baking the package. The end result is a soft, slightly sweet bread with a delicious fresh corn flavor. Kneel-down bread gets its name from being baked in a pit oven. The cook had to kneel down to do the baking. To make this dish, you must have fresh corn picked that day.

6 ears fresh corn, unhusked
1 4-ounce can green chilies, seeded and chopped
1 egg, beaten

Preheat the oven to 350°.

Husk the ears, discarding the silk and tough outer husks but reserving the inner husks.

With a sharp knife, cut the kernels from the cob. Using the back of the knife, scrape the cobs to extract the additional corn bits and milk.

Combine the corn kernels and scraped corn in a mixing bowl. Add the green chilies and egg and mix well.

Spread the reserved corn husks flat on a work surface. Overlap them by half to form a rectangle approximately 7 × 12 inches. Mound the corn mixture in the middle of the rectangle and form it into a loaf shape. Fold the husks over the corn mixture to make a package. Use two pieces of string to tie the package closed widthwise and lengthwise. Place on a baking sheet and bake until the loaf is cooked through and firm, about 60 to 75 minutes. To serve, place the package on a serving dish. Cut the strings, fold back the corn husks, and slice.

Serves 4 to 6

Iroquois Strawberry Bread

The Strawberry Festival is an important thanksgiving celebration among the Iroquois. This bread is a traditional dish during that observance. You can find hazelnut butter at gourmet shops and health-food stores.

1/3 cup hazelnut butter
1 3/4 cups water
1/2 cup honey
1 cup cornmeal
1 cup flour
1 teaspoon baking soda
1/2 teaspoon salt
1 cup halved fresh strawberries

Preheat the oven to 375°.

In a small saucepan, combine the hazelnut butter and the water. Bring to a boil over moderate heat, stirring occasionally, then immediately remove from the heat. Stir in the honey and set aside to cool.

Combine the cornmeal, flour, baking soda, and salt in a mixing bowl. Mix well. Pour in the nut mixture and mix well. Gently stir in the strawberries.

Pour the batter into a greased loaf pan. Bake until a knife inserted into the center comes out clean, about 30 to 35 minutes.

Serves 6

Boston Brown Bread

Boston brown bread is steamed, not baked. The simplest way to steam the bread is to use coffee cans set on a rack inside a very large pot or steamer. If you still have the plastic lids for the cans, so much the better. This recipe makes two loaves if you use 1-pound coffee cans; if you use larger or smaller cans, it will make proportionately fewer or more loaves and take more or less time to steam.

1½ cups whole wheat flour
½ cup rye flour
1 cup yellow cornmeal
1½ teaspoons baking soda
1½ teaspoons baking powder
1 teaspoon salt
1 egg
2 tablespoons vegetable oil
2 cups buttermilk
¼ cup milk
½ cup molasses
1 cup dark raisins

Lightly grease the coffee cans and dust them with flour.

Combine the whole wheat flour, rye flour, cornmeal, baking soda, baking powder, and salt in a large mixing bowl. Mix well.

In another mixing bowl, beat together the egg, vegetable oil, buttermilk, milk, and molasses. Mix well. Stir in the raisins. Pour the mixture into the dry ingredients and stir until they are just mixed.

Fill the coffee cans two-thirds full with the batter. If you have the lids, cover the cans with them. If not, cover the cans with heavy aluminum foil and tie it in place with string.

Put a steaming rack in the bottom of a pot or steamer large enough to hold the cans. Fill the pot with very hot water until it comes two-thirds of the way up the cans. Cover the pot and bring the water to a boil over moderate heat. Reduce the heat to low and simmer, covered, until a cake tester inserted into the center of the bread comes out clean. This will take about 1½ hours if you use small cans, and about 2 to 3 hours if you use larger cans. Let the cans cool, uncovered, until the bread slides out easily, about 30 to 45 minutes, before serving.

Makes 2 loaves

ANADAMA BREAD

The legend behind the name is: A New England farmer's wife named Anna was equally renowned for her cooking and her bad temper. When she left home in a huff, her husband had to make her bread recipe himself, muttering all the while, "Anna, damn her."

2 cups milk
1 cup water
4 tablespoons unsalted butter
1 cup cornmeal
5 to 6 cups flour
½ cup molasses
2 packages (2 tablespoons) active dry yeast
1 tablespoon salt

In a 2-quart saucepan over moderate heat, combine the milk, water, and butter. Cook until the mixture just boils, then immediately remove the saucepan from the heat. Using a wooden spoon, gradually add the cornmeal, stirring until the mixture is smooth. Pour the mixture into a large mixing bowl and let stand until lukewarm.

Using a wooden spoon, stir in 1 cup of the flour and the molasses, yeast, and salt. Stir in 4 more cups of flour, about half a cup at a time. The dough should be very stiff; add more flour if needed.

Turn the dough out onto a floured surface and knead until the dough is quite stiff and not at all sticky, about 10 minutes. Place the dough in a greased bowl and cover with plastic wrap. Let the dough rise in a warm place until doubled in bulk, about 1 to 1½ hours.

Preheat the oven to 350°.

Punch the dough down and form it into a round loaf about 6 inches in diameter. Place the loaf on a lightly greased baking sheet and bake until it is browned on top and bottom and sounds hollow when tapped, about 50 minutes. Cool on a wire rack.

Makes 1 loaf

Cornmeal Yeast Rolls

2 packages (2 tablespoons) active dry yeast
2 teaspoons salt
¼ cup honey
2 cups very warm water (about 110°)
½ cup vegetable oil
2 cups yellow cornmeal
5 to 6 cups flour

In a large mixing bowl, combine the yeast, salt, honey, and warm water. Stir well to dissolve the yeast. Stir in the oil. Add the cornmeal and stir well. Using a wooden spoon, stir in 5 cups of the flour, about half a cup at a time. The dough should be soft but not sticky; add more flour if needed.

Turn the dough out onto a floured surface and knead until smooth and elastic, about 10 minutes. Place the dough is a greased bowl and cover with plastic wrap. Let the dough rise in a warm place until doubled in bulk, about 1 hour.

Punch down the dough and knead it briefly, about 1 minute. Roll out the dough about ½ inch thick. Cut the dough into 2-inch squares. Fold the squares in half and place them on a lightly greased baking sheet. Cover with plastic wrap and let rise again in a warm place until doubled in bulk, about 30 minutes.

Preheat the oven to 375°.

Bake until the rolls are browned on top, about 15 minutes. Serve hot.

Makes about 4 dozen rolls

RYE 'N' INJUN BREAD

In colonial times, wheat was scarce, but rye flour and cornmeal ("Injun" meal) were plentiful—hence this dense loaf.

1½ cup very warm water (about 110°)
1 package (1 tablespoon) active dry yeast
3 tablespoons molasses
2 tablespoons unsalted butter, softened
2 teaspoons salt
2 cups yellow cornmeal
2 cups rye flour
1½ to 2 cups flour

Place the water in a large mixing bowl. Sprinkle the yeast into the water and let stand until foamy, about 5 minutes. Using a wooden spoon, stir in the molasses, butter, and salt. Stir in the cornmeal and rye flour, half a cup at a time. Stir in the flour, half a cup at a time (knead with your hands when the dough becomes too thick to stir with the spoon). Add enough flour to make a stiff dough that is not sticky.

Turn the dough out onto a floured surface and knead until it is smooth and elastic, about 10 minutes. Add more flour if the dough becomes sticky. Place the dough in a greased bowl and cover with plastic wrap. Let the dough rise in a warm place until it is about 1½ times bigger in bulk, about 2 hours.

Punch the dough down and knead it again on a floured surface until it is elastic, about 5 to 10 minutes. Divide the dough in half and form each half into a round loaf. Using a serrated knife, slash an *X* across the top of each loaf. Place the loaves about 6 inches apart on a baking sheet. Cover with plastic wrap and let rise again in a warm place for about 45 to 60 minutes.

Preheat the oven to 375°.

Bake the loaves until they are browned on top and bottom and sound hollow when tapped, about 45 minutes. Let cool completely on a wire rack before slicing.

Makes 2 loaves

Masa Harina Bread

Finely ground masa harina is used to make tortillas. When used in this recipe, the masa harina makes a dense, crusty loaf.

1¼ cups very warm water (about 110°)
1 tablespoon sugar
1 package (1 tablespoon) active dry yeast
2 to 2½ cups flour
1 teaspoon salt
1 cup masa harina

Place the water in a large mixing bowl and stir in the sugar. Sprinkle the yeast into the water and let stand until foamy, about 5 minutes.

Using a wooden spoon, stir in 1 cup of the flour and the salt. Stir in the masa harina and mix well. Stir in 1½ cups more flour, half a cup at a time. The dough should be stiff and not sticky; add more flour if needed.

Turn the dough out onto a floured surface and knead until it is smooth and elastic, about 10 minutes. Add more flour if the dough becomes sticky. Place the dough is a greased bowl and cover with plastic wrap. Let the dough rise in a warm place until it is doubled in bulk, about 1½ to 2 hours.

Punch the dough down and knead it again on a floured surface until it is elastic, about 5 minutes. Shape the dough into a round loaf about 6 inches in diameter. Place the loaf in a 9-inch baking dish, cover with plastic wrap, and let rise in a warm place again until doubled in bulk, about 45 to 60 minutes.

Using a serrated knife, slash an *X* across the top of the loaf.

Preheat the oven to 375°.

Bake until the loaf is browned on top and bottom and sounds hollow when tapped, about 30 to 35 minutes. Let cool completely on a wire rack before slicing.

Makes 1 loaf

Cornbread Stuffing

This is the traditional way to use up leftover cornbread. This recipe makes enough to stuff a medium turkey (about 12 to 14 pounds) or two large chickens. To serve stuffing as a side dish, put it into a greased baking dish and bake, covered, at 350° for about 1 hour. For a crispier top, uncover for the last 15 minutes of baking.

4 tablespoons unsalted butter
1 large onion, chopped
2 celery stalks, chopped
2 garlic cloves, finely chopped
4 cups crumbled stale cornbread
1 tablespoon dried parsley
½ teaspoon dried thyme
¼ teaspoon dried sage
½ teaspoon salt
freshly ground black pepper to taste
1 cup chicken broth

Melt the butter in a skillet over moderate heat. Add the onion, celery, and garlic and cook, stirring often, until the onion is softened, about 5 minutes.

In a large mixing bowl combine the cornbread, parsley, thyme, sage, salt, and lots of black pepper. Add the onion mixture and toss until the ingredients are well blended. Stir in the chicken broth, a little at a time, until the ingredients are well moistened but not soggy (use less than 1 cup broth if possible).

Makes about 6 cups

Cornbread Stuffing with Sausage

1 pound hot Italian sausages
4 tablespoons unsalted butter
1 large onion, chopped
2 celery stalks, chopped
2 garlic cloves, finely chopped
4 cups crumbled stale cornbread
1 tablespoon dried parsley
1/2 teaspoon dried thyme
1/4 teaspoon dried sage
1/2 teaspoon salt
freshly ground black pepper to taste
1 cup coarsely chopped pecans
1 cup chicken broth

Remove the sausage meat from the casings. In a large skillet, cook the meat over moderate heat, stirring often to break up large lumps, until it is lightly browned, about 10 minutes. Using a slotted spoon, remove the sausage meat and set aside in a large mixing bowl.

Add the butter to the sausage drippings in the skillet. When it is melted, add the onion, celery, and garlic and cook, stirring often, until the onion is softened, about 5 minutes.

Add the onion mixture to the mixing bowl with the sausage. Add the cornbread, parsley, thyme, sage, salt, and lots of black pepper. Toss until the ingredients are well blended. Add the pecans and toss again. Stir in the chicken broth, a little at a time, until the ingredients are well moistened but not soggy (use less than 1 cup broth if possible).

Makes about 8 cups

CHAPTER

10

Corn on the Griddle

The recipes below are all unleavened, thin cakes that are quickly cooked on the stove top using a griddle or heavy skillet. Some of the most traditional cornmeal preparations—johnnycakes, corn oysters, hushpuppies—are found here. Try the pancake variations as a flavorful alternative to wheat-based pancakes.

Cornmeal Pancakes

2 eggs
2 cups milk
1 cup yellow cornmeal
1 teaspoon sugar
1/4 teaspoon salt
6 tablespoons unsalted butter, melted

Whisk the eggs in a mixing bowl until light. Whisk in the milk, cornmeal, sugar, salt, and butter. Continue to beat until mixture is smooth.

Lightly grease a griddle or heavy skillet. Heat over moderate heat until quite hot. Drop about 3 tablespoonfuls of batter per pancake on the griddle, being careful not to let the pancakes touch (cook the pancakes in batches, stirring the batter well each time). Cook until bubbles form on the top and the pancakes are golden brown on the bottom, about 3 to 4 minutes. Flip the pancakes over and cook on the other side until lightly browned, about 3 to 4 minutes longer.

Makes 12 pancakes

Cornmeal Flapjacks

1 1/2 cups yellow cornmeal
2 1/2 cups flour
4 teaspoons baking powder
1/4 cup sugar
1 teaspoon salt
1/8 teaspoon ground nutmeg
1 egg, beaten
2/3 cup milk
1/4 cup corn oil

Combine the cornmeal, flour, baking powder, sugar, salt, and nutmeg in a mixing bowl. Mix well. Add the egg, milk, and oil and stir until the ingredients are just mixed; the batter will still be a little lumpy.

Heat an ungreased griddle or large, heavy skillet over moderate heat until quite hot. Drop about 3 tablespoonfuls of batter per flapjack on the griddle, being careful not to let the flapjacks touch (cook the flapjacks in batches, stirring the batter well each time). Cook until bubbles form on the top and the flapjacks are golden brown on the bottom, about 3 to 4 minutes. Flip the flapjacks over and cook on the other side until lightly browned, about 3 to 4 minutes longer.

Makes about 24 flapjacks

Corn Griddlecakes

2 cups yellow cornmeal
¼ cup flour
1 package (1 tablespoon) active dry yeast
2 teaspoons sugar
½ teaspoon salt
2 cups milk

Combine the cornmeal, flour, yeast, sugar, and salt in a mixing bowl. Add the milk and stir until the mixture is smooth. Let stand for 15 minutes.

Lightly grease a griddle or heavy skillet. Heat over moderate heat until quite hot. Drop about 3 tablespoonfuls of batter per griddlecake on the griddle, being careful not to let the cakes touch (cook the griddlecakes in batches, stirring the batter well each time). Cook until bubbles form on the top and the griddlecakes are golden brown on the bottom, about 3 to 4 minutes. Flip the griddlecakes over and cook on the other side until lightly browned, about 3 to 4 minutes longer.

Makes 10 to 12 griddlecakes

Fresh Corn Griddlecakes

2 cups corn kernels
1 cup light cream or half-and-half
2 tablespoons unsalted butter, melted
2 eggs
1 cup flour
½ teaspoon salt
1 tablespoon sugar
2 teaspoons baking powder

In a food processor or blender combine the corn kernels, light cream, butter, and eggs. Process briefly, just until the mixture is blended. Do not puree.

Pour the corn mixture into a mixing bowl. Add the flour, salt, sugar, and baking powder and mix well.

Lightly grease a griddle or heavy skillet. Heat over moderate heat until quite hot. Drop about 3 tablespoonfuls of batter per cake on the griddle, being careful not to let the cakes touch (cook in batches). Cook until the cakes are puffed on top and golden brown on the bottom, about 3 to 4 minutes. Flip the cakes over and cook on the other side until lightly browned, about 3 to 4 minutes longer.

Makes 10 to 12 griddlecakes

Cornmeal Waffles

1 cup cornmeal
1 cup flour
2 teaspoons baking powder
1 teaspoon baking soda
1 teaspoon sugar
½ teaspoon salt

2 eggs
1 cup buttermilk
1 cup sour cream
1/3 cup corn oil

Heat the waffle iron.

Combine the cornmeal, flour, baking powder, baking soda, sugar, and salt in a mixing bowl. Mix well.

In another mixing bowl, beat together the eggs, buttermilk, sour cream, and corn oil. Pour the mixture into the dry ingredients and stir well until smooth. Do not overmix.

Pour about 3/4 cup of the batter onto the heated waffle iron and cook until golden brown, about 5 minutes.

Makes 6 to 8 waffles

Fried Tomato Cakes

2 large, ripe tomatoes, seeded and diced
3 scallions, thinly sliced
salt to taste
freshly ground black pepper to taste
1 cup yellow cornmeal
1/2 cup corn oil

Combine the tomatoes and scallions in a mixing bowl and season to taste with salt and black pepper. Add the cornmeal and mix well. Shape the mixture with your hands into 10 small patties.

Heat the corn oil in a large, heavy skillet over moderate heat until it is very hot. Add the patties (in batches if necessary) and cook until golden on the bottom, about 2 to 3 minutes. Flip the patties over and cook until golden on the other side, about 2 to 3 minutes longer. Add additional oil to the skillet if needed. Drain on paper towels.

Makes about 10 cakes

Corn Cakes with Goat Cheese

$\frac{1}{4}$ cup sun-dried tomatoes
$\frac{1}{2}$ cup yellow cornmeal
$\frac{1}{2}$ cup flour
$\frac{1}{2}$ teaspoon baking powder
$\frac{1}{2}$ teaspoon salt
$\frac{1}{4}$ teaspoon hot red pepper flakes
freshly ground black pepper to taste
1 cup corn kernels
1 garlic clove, finely chopped
1 cup milk
$\frac{1}{3}$ cup crumbled mild goat cheese
1 tablespoon olive oil
1 egg
$\frac{1}{4}$ cup vegetable oil

Place the sun-dried tomatoes in a small bowl and add enough boiling water to cover. Soak until tomatoes are softened, about 10 minutes. Drain and chop.

Combine the cornmeal, flour, baking powder, salt, red pepper flakes, and lots of black pepper in a mixing bowl. Stir well. Add the tomatoes, corn kernels, and garlic and stir well.

Combine the milk, goat cheese, olive oil, and egg in a food processor or blender. Process until smooth. Pour the mixture into the corn mixture and stir until the ingredients are just combined. Do not overmix. Let stand for 15 minutes.

Heat the oil in a large, heavy skillet over moderate heat. Spoon about 2 tablespoons of batter per cake into the skillet. Do not crowd the cakes; cook in batches if necessary. Cook until the tops of the cakes are bubbly and the edges are just beginning to brown, about 2 to 3 minutes. Flip the cakes over and cook until browned on the other side, about 2 minutes more.

Makes about 18 cakes

Cornmeal Bannock

1½ cups cornmeal
½ cup water
4 tablespoons unsalted butter, melted
4 tablespoons pure maple syrup
¼ cup corn oil

Combine the cornmeal, water, butter, and maple syrup in a mixing bowl. Stir well until smooth.

Heat half the oil in a large, heavy skillet over moderate heat until it is very hot. Drop the batter by tablespoonfuls into the skillet, being careful not to let the bannocks touch (cook the bannocks in batches if necessary). Press down on the bannocks with a spatula and cook until they are golden brown and crispy on the bottom, about 3 to 4 minutes. Flip the bannocks over and cook on the other side until lightly browned, about 3 to 4 minutes longer. Add more oil to the skillet as needed.

Serves 4

Dropped Cornmeal Scones

Dropped scones are made using a batter that is dropped onto a hot griddle.

⅓ cup cornmeal
⅔ cup flour
½ teaspoon sugar
½ teaspoon baking soda
½ teaspoon baking powder
½ teaspoon salt

1 egg

½ cup buttermilk

corn oil for greasing skillet

In a medium mixing bowl, combine the cornmeal, flour, sugar, baking soda, baking powder, and salt.

In another bowl, beat together the egg and buttermilk. Add the liquid to the cornmeal mixture and stir until just mixed. Do not overmix.

Lightly grease a large griddle or skillet with the corn oil and heat over medium heat. When the griddle is hot, drop the batter by tablespoons onto it and cook about 1 minute per side, or until the scones puff up and are golden brown. Serve hot with jam.

Makes 18 to 24 scones

JOHNNYCAKES

1 cup white cornmeal

1 teaspoon sugar

1 teaspoon salt

1½ cups boiling water

Combine the cornmeal, sugar, and salt in a mixing bowl. Quickly add the boiling water, stirring constantly, to make a smooth, very thick batter.

Heat a well-greased, large, heavy griddle or skillet over moderate heat until very hot. Drop the batter by tablespoonfuls onto the griddle and smooth them to about ½ inch thick. Don't let the cakes touch (cook in batches if necessary). Cook until the cakes are browned on the bottom, about 5 minutes. Flip the cakes over and cook on the other side until browned, about 5 minutes longer. Serve hot.

Makes about 8 to 10 cakes

Wild Rice Johnnycakes

Wild rice has long been a staple food for the Native American peoples of the Great Lakes region. Today wild rice is gathered by members of the Chippewa and Menominee tribes.

3/4 cup wild rice
1 1/2 cups water
1/2 teaspoon salt
3 tablespoons cornmeal
3 tablespoons bacon drippings

Rinse the wild rice well in running water.

Combine the wild rice, water, and salt in a 2-quart saucepan. Bring to a boil over moderate heat. Reduce the heat slightly and cook until the water is absorbed and the rice is tender, about 30 to 35 minutes.

Stir in the cornmeal and let the mixture cool.

When cool enough to handle, form the mixture into cakes about 3 inches in diameter.

Heat the bacon drippings in a large, heavy skillet over moderate heat. When very hot, add the cakes (in batches if necessary) and cook until golden brown on the bottom, about 2 to 3 minutes. Flip the cakes over and cook until golden brown on the other side, about 2 to 3 minutes longer. Serve hot.

Makes about 8 to 10 cakes

Hushpuppies

Tradition has it that hushpuppies were invented at a fish fry to quiet some hungry, yelping dogs. Leftover cornmeal batter was cooked in leftover hot lard, then thrown to the dogs with the words, "Hush,puppies!" Is there any truth to this legend? Does it matter?

Hushpuppies are improvisational by definition. For a spicier version, add a dash of cayenne pepper. For a more filling version, add half a cup of shredded Cheddar or Monterey Jack cheese. For a trendier version, add half a cup of mild goat cheese. For a variation that goes well with roasted meats, add a pinch of dried thyme.

½ cup cornmeal
6 tablespoons flour
½ teaspoon baking powder
½ teaspoon baking soda
¼ teaspoon salt
¼ cup finely chopped onion
1/3 cup corn kernels
½ cup buttermilk
about 1 cup vegetable oil for frying

Stir together the cornmeal, flour, baking powder, baking soda, and salt in a mixing bowl. Stir in the onion and corn kernels. Stir in the buttermilk and mix until just combined.

Add the vegetable oil to a large cast-iron skillet or heavy skillet to a depth of ¼ inch. Heat the oil over medium-high heat until it just begins to smoke. Drop the batter by teaspoonfuls into the hot oil, being careful not to crowd them in the skillet (cook the hushpuppies in batches if necessary). Cook, turning several times, until the hushpuppies are golden brown, about 2½ to 3 minutes. Lower the heat if the oil becomes too hot; carefully add more oil to the skillet if necessary. Drain on paper towels and serve hot.

Makes about 30 hushpuppies

CAJUN SWEET HUSHPUPPIES

1 cup flour
½ cup sugar
½ cup yellow cornmeal
2 tablespoons baking powder

¼ teaspoon salt

⅛ teaspoon cayenne pepper

1 large onion, very finely chopped

1 medium green bell pepper, seeded and very finely chopped

6 scallions (green parts only), very finely chopped

1 egg, beaten

about 1 cup vegetable oil for frying

Combine the flour, sugar, cornmeal, baking powder, salt, and cayenne pepper in a large mixing bowl. Mix well. Add the onion, green pepper, scallions, and egg. Mix well again to form a dry batter. Cover the bowl and refrigerate for 2 hours.

Add the vegetable oil to a large cast-iron or heavy skillet to a depth of ½ inch. Heat the oil over medium-high heat until it just begins to smoke. Drop the batter by tablespoonfuls into the hot oil, being careful not to crowd them in the skillet (cook the hushpuppies in batches if necessary). Cook, turning several times, until the hushpuppies are golden brown, about 2½ to 3 minutes. Lower the heat if the oil becomes too hot; carefully add more oil to the skillet if necessary. Drain on paper towels and serve hot.

Makes about 30 hushpuppies

Corn Oysters

Corn oysters—a fanciful name for plain old corn fritters—are delicate, crispy morsels made of corn kernels (the fresher the better) held together with a light batter and then quickly fried in hot oil. For a more savory flavor, add a large pinch of chopped fresh basil, parsley, or other herb along with a tablespoon or two of finely chopped onion. For a spicier flavor, add a pinch of cayenne pepper.

Some recipes for corn fritters use considerably more flour relative to the corn kernels than is called for here. In an attempt to lighten the inevitably heavy result, those recipes then add baking powder. The final result is a doughy fritter that must be fried for so long that greasiness is certain. Avoid those recipes—your digestion will thank you.

2 eggs, separated
2 cups corn kernels
4 tablespoons flour
2 tablespoons unsalted butter, melted
1 teaspoon sugar
1/2 teaspoon salt
about 1/2 cup vegetable oil for frying

Beat the egg yolks in a mixing bowl. Add the corn kernels, flour, butter, sugar, and salt. Mix well.

In another bowl, beat the egg whites until they are stiff but not dry. Fold the whites into the corn mixture.

Add the vegetable oil to a large cast-iron or heavy skillet to a depth of about 1 inch. Heat the oil over medium-high heat until it just begins to smoke. Drop the batter by tablespoonfuls into the hot oil, being careful not to crowd them in the skillet (cook the fritters in batches if necessary). Cook, turning several times, until the fritters are golden brown and crispy, about 5 to 6 minutes. Lower the heat if the oil becomes too hot; carefully add more oil to the skillet if necessary. Drain on paper towels and serve hot.

Makes about 16 to 20 fritters

Corn and Shrimp Fritters

1/2 pound shrimp, peeled and cleaned
1 cup corn kernels
3 tablespoons milk
1 small onion, finely chopped
1 egg
1/2 teaspoon salt
1/8 teaspoon cayenne pepper
1/3 cup yellow cornmeal
about 1/2 cup vegetable oil for frying

Coarsely chop the shrimp. In a food processor, combine the shrimp, corn, milk, onion, and egg. Process briefly, just enough to blend the ingredients but not puree them.

Pour the shrimp mixture into a mixing bowl. Add the salt, cayenne, and cornmeal and mix well. Let stand for 20 to 30 minutes.

Add the vegetable oil to a large cast-iron or heavy skillet to a depth of 1/4 inch. Heat the oil over medium-high heat until it just begins to smoke. Drop the batter by tablespoonfuls into the hot oil, being careful not to crowd them in the skillet (cook the fritters in batches if necessary). Cook until the fritters are golden brown on the bottom, about 2 1/2 to 3 minutes. Turn the fritters over and cook on the other side until golden brown, about 2 1/2 to 3 minutes longer. Lower the heat if the oil becomes too hot; carefully add more oil to the skillet if necessary. Drain on paper towels and serve hot.

Makes about 16 to 20 fritters

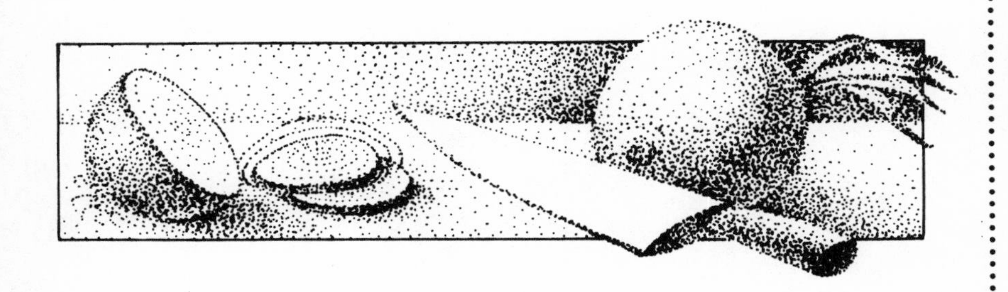

CHAPTER
11

Desserts

Because corn is inherently sweet, it's no surprise that there are a lot of great corn-based desserts. ✂ *Because cornmeal is low in gluten, it's also no surprise that few of these desserts are cakes or cookies.* ✂ *What may surprise some is that soft, creamy puddings made from commercial mixes contain corn as well, in the form of cornstarch.*

Indian Pudding

This venerable old dessert has deep New England roots. It's best served warm, topped with heavy cream, whipped cream, maple syrup, or ice cream.

½ cup yellow cornmeal
½ cup dark, unsulphured molasses
¼ cup sugar
½ cup dark raisins
½ teaspoon salt
½ teaspoon ground ginger
½ teaspoon cinnamon
½ teaspoon ground cloves
½ teaspoon ground nutmeg
4 cups milk
4 tablespoons unsalted butter, softened
1 cup heavy cream

Preheat the oven to 300°.

Combine the cornmeal, molasses, sugar, raisins, salt, ginger, cinnamon, cloves, and nutmeg in a mixing bowl. Stir well to break up any lumps.

Heat the milk in a heavy 2-quart saucepan over moderate heat until it is very hot but not boiling. Slowly whisk the milk, about ¼ cup at a time, into the cornmeal mixture. Stir in the butter.

Pour the mixture back into the saucepan and cook over moderate heat, stirring constantly, until the mixture thickens, about 5 minutes.

Pour the mixture into a greased 2-quart baking dish. Bake for 1 hour. Pour the cream evenly over the top of the pudding *(do not stir)* and bake until the cream has been absorbed and the top is golden brown, about 3 hours longer.

Serves 6

Sattoo

This sweet corn pudding from northwestern India is traditionally served as a breakfast dish or snack. To Western palates, it makes a satisfying, not-too-sweet dessert.

1½ cups white cornmeal
6 tablespoons unsalted butter, melted
4 cups water
¾ cup light brown sugar
¼ cup raisins
½ cup crushed unsalted pistachio nuts
2 cups sliced fresh fruit and/or berries

Combine the cornmeal and melted butter in a heavy, 2-quart saucepan and mix well with a wooden spoon.

Cook over medium heat, stirring constantly, until the cornmeal is glazed and darkened, about 10 minutes. Quickly stir in the water. Continue to cook, stirring constantly, until all the water is absorbed, about 20 minutes. Stir in the brown sugar and continue to cook until it is all absorbed. Turn off the heat and stir in the raisins.

Spread the crushed pistachios in the bottom of 9-inch round pie plate. Spread the warm pudding on top of the pistachios and let cool.

To serve, invert the pudding onto a platter and surround it with the fruit. Cut into wedges.

Serves 6

Vanilla Pudding

Simple puddings of milk thickened with cornstarch have long been favorite American desserts. Nowadays most home cooks use packaged pudding mixes. But since these mixes consist basically of just cornstarch, sugar, and flavorings, why not make pudding yourself? To prevent the pudding from breaking down after cooking, measure accurately and make sure the mixture reaches the right temperature for thorough cooking.

3 tablespoons cornstarch
1/3 cup sugar
1/8 teaspoon salt
2 1/4 cups milk
1 teaspoon pure vanilla extract

Combine the cornstarch, sugar, salt, and 1/4 cup of the milk in a heavy, 2-quart saucepan. Stir well.

In another saucepan, bring the remaining 2 cups milk just to a boil and immediately remove from the heat. Slowly pour the milk into the cornstarch mixture, whisking constantly.

Cook the pudding over low heat, stirring constantly, until the mixture thickens and is very hot (195° on a candy thermometer). Cover the saucepan and cook 10 minutes.

Remove from the heat, stir in the vanilla, cover, and let cool. Pour the mixture into a serving dish or small individual bowls, cover with plastic wrap, and chill before serving.

Serves 4

Chocolate Pudding

1/4 cup unsweetened dark cocoa
1/2 cup sugar
3 tablespoons cornstarch
1/8 teaspoon salt
2 cups milk
1 teaspoon pure vanilla extract

Combine the cocoa, sugar, cornstarch, and salt in a heavy, 2-quart saucepan. Slowly pour in the milk, stirring constantly to break up any lumps.

Cook the pudding over low heat, stirring constantly, until the mixture thickens and is very hot (195° on a candy thermometer). Cover the saucepan and cook 5 minutes longer.

Remove from the heat, stir in the vanilla, cover, and let cool. Pour the mixture into a serving dish or small individual bowls, cover with plastic wrap, and chill before serving.

Serves 4

BLUEBERRY CORN COBBLER

1/3 cup milk
1 egg
2 tablespoons unsalted butter, melted
1 teaspoon baking powder
1/2 teaspoon salt
1 1/4 cups yellow cornmeal
3/4 cup honey
4 cups fresh or frozen (unthawed) blueberries

Preheat the oven to 375°.

Beat the milk, egg, butter, baking powder, and salt in a mixing bowl. Add the cornmeal and 1/2 cup of the honey, stirring well to break up any lumps.

Spread the berries in the bottom of a 9-inch baking dish. Drizzle the remaining honey over the berries.

Drop the batter by tablespoonfuls over the berries. Bake until the crust is golden brown and the berries are bubbling, about 30 to 35 minutes.

Serves 4

Simple Cornmeal Cake

Serve this lemony cake topped with fresh berries and a spoonful of maple syrup.

1 cup yellow cornmeal
1/2 cup flour
1 1/2 teaspoons baking powder
1/2 teaspoon salt
1 cup sugar
1/4 cup corn oil
2 tablespoons unsalted butter, softened
3 eggs
1/2 cup plain, low-fat yogurt
grated zest of 1 lemon
1 tablespoon lemon juice

Preheat the oven to 350°. Line the bottom of a 10-inch round cake pan with waxed paper.

Combine the cornmeal, flour, baking powder, and salt in a mixing bowl.

In another mixing bowl, whisk together the sugar, corn oil, and butter. Beat in the eggs one at a time, stirring briefly after each addition. Stir in the yogurt. Add the lemon zest and lemon juice and stir again. Add the cornmeal mixture and stir just until well combined. Do not overmix.

Pour the batter into the cake pan and bake until the cake is golden brown and a toothpick inserted into the center comes out clean, about 40 minutes. Let cool for 10 minutes in the pan, then invert onto a wire rack and let cool completely.

Makes 1 cake

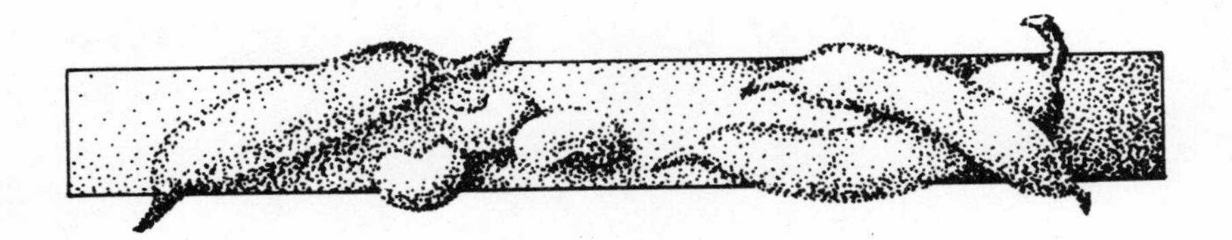

CORNMEAL PLUM CAKE

The small, purple prune plums that are in season in the early fall are ideal for this cake.

1 pound small fresh plums
1 cup yellow cornmeal
3/4 cup whole wheat flour
1 1/2 teaspoons baking powder
1/4 cup honey
1 egg, beaten
grated zest of 1 lemon
4 to 5 tablespoons milk
confectioner's sugar

Preheat the oven to 375°. Line a 7 × 11-inch cake pan with waxed paper.

Halve the plums and remove the pits. Set aside.

Combine the cornmeal, flour, and baking powder in a mixing bowl. Add the honey, egg, and lemon zest and stir well. Stir in the milk, 1 tablespoon at a time, until a soft dough is formed.

Spread the dough in the cake pan. Arrange the plum halves, cut-side down, on the top. Bake until golden brown, about 20 to 25 minutes. Dust with confectioner's sugar and serve warm.

Makes 1 cake

MAPLE PECAN COFFECAKE

8 tablespoons (1 stick) unsalted butter, softened
1 cup sugar
3 eggs
1 teaspoon pure vanilla extract
1/2 cup yellow cornmeal

1½ cups flour

2 teaspoons baking soda

½ teaspoon salt

⅔ cup buttermilk

1 cup finely chopped pecans

¾ cup maple syrup

Preheat the oven to 350°.

In a large mixing bowl, cream together the butter and sugar until pale and fluffy. Add the eggs, one at a time, beating well after each addition. Beat in the vanilla.

In another bowl, combine the cornmeal, flour, baking soda, and salt. Mix well. Add about a third of the cornmeal mixture to the butter mixture and beat well. Add ⅓ cup buttermilk and beat well. Add another third of the cornmeal mixture and beat well. Add the remaining buttermilk and beat well. Add the remaining cornmeal mixture and beat well again. Stir in the chopped nuts and mix well.

Pour the batter into a greased 9 × 13-inch baking pan. Bake until firm and lightly browned, about 30 minutes. Remove the cake from the oven and pour the maple syrup over the top. Return to the oven and bake 5 minutes longer. Let cool completely before serving.

Makes 1 cake

Cornmeal Butter Cookies

½ pound (2 sticks) unsalted butter, softened

1 cup confectioner's sugar

1½ teaspoons pure vanilla extract

½ teaspoons grated lemon zest

¼ teaspoon salt

2 eggs

2 cups flour

1½ cups yellow cornmeal

Preheat the oven to 350°.

In a large mixing bowl, cream together the butter and sugar until pale and fluffy. Beat in the vanilla, lemon zest, and salt. Add the eggs, one at a time, beating well after each addition. Beat in the flour and 1 cup of the cornmeal.

Place the remaining ½ cup cornmeal on a flat plate. Form the dough into small balls about ¾-inch in diameter. Roll each ball in the cornmeal until it is well coated. Flatten the balls between your hands into rounds about 2 inches in diameter and ¼ inch thick. Arrange the rounds on two lightly greased cookie sheets, leaving about 2 inches between each round.

Bake until the cookies are lightly browned around the edges, about 20 to 25 minutes. Cool completely on wire racks.

Makes about 4 dozen cookies

Sweet Corn Pudding

This rich pudding is a traditional favorite in Costa Rica.

3 cups corn kernels
½ cup milk
8 ounces farmer's cheese, crumbled
½ cup sugar
2 eggs, beaten
1 tablespoon unsalted butter, melted

Preheat the oven to 350°.

Place the corn kernels in a food processor or blender and process until finely ground. Pour the kernels into a mixing bowl and stir in the milk. Add the farmer's cheese, sugar, eggs, and butter. Beat well.

Pour the mixture into a greased 8-inch baking dish and bake until lightly browned on top, about 40 minutes. Serve warm or at room temperature.

Serves 4

Corn and Blueberry Pudding

3 cups corn kernels
2 cups fresh or frozen (not thawed) blueberries
3 tablespoons cornstarch
½ cup sugar
¼ teaspoon ground nutmeg
3 eggs, separated
1 cup plain low-fat yogurt
4 tablespoons unsalted butter, melted

Combine the corn, blueberries, cornstarch, sugar, and nutmeg in a mixing bowl. Toss well.

In another bowl, beat the egg yolks together with the yogurt. Pour the mixture over the corn. Add the butter and mix well.

In another bowl, beat the egg whites until they are stiff but not dry. Gently stir the egg whites into the corn mixture.

Pour the pudding into a greased 2-quart baking dish and bake until firm and lightly browned on top, about 35 to 45 minutes. Let stand 10 minutes before serving.

Serves 4

Buñuelos with Syrup

This simple dessert of corn dumplings in a rich syrup is a favorite in Latin America. For true Mexican flavor, be sure to use the anise.

4 cups masa harina
2 eggs, beaten
4 ounces crumbled farmer cheese
½ cup vegetable oil

SYRUP

2 cups brown sugar
½ cup water
1 2-inch piece cinnamon
1 star anise pod (optional)

Combine the masa harina, eggs, and farmer cheese in a mixing bowl. Stir well until smooth.

To make the dumplings, form heaping teaspoons of the dough into round balls, then flatten them between your hands to make rounds about ¼ inch thick and 1½ inches in diameter.

To make the syrup, combine the brown sugar, water, cinnamon, and anise in a heavy, 2-quart saucepan. Cook over low heat, stirring often, until the mixture resembles maple syrup, about 15 to 20 minutes.

Heat the vegetable oil in a large, heavy skillet over moderate heat. Add the dumplings (in batches if necessary) and cook until lightly browned on the bottom, about 1 to 2 minutes. Flip the dumplings over and cook until lightly browned on the other side, about 1 to 2 minutes longer. Add the cooked dumplings to the simmering syrup and cook for 5 minutes longer, counting from the time the last dumpling is added.

Remove the saucepan from the heat and let the dumplings soak in the syrup for 30 minutes before serving.

Makes about 20 dumplings

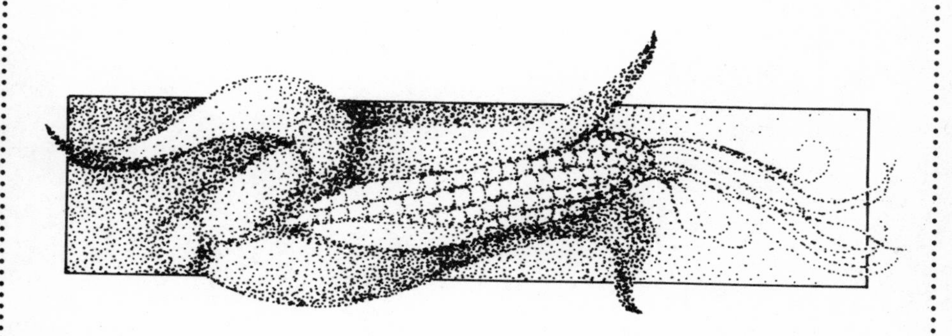

Chapter 12

Condiments, Relishes, and Preserves

Corn adds color, crunch, and flavor to condiments, relishes, and preserves. Quick corn relishes can be made year-round using fresh, canned, or frozen corn. Corn preserves should be made only with the freshest possible corn at the height of the season. When you eat them over the winter, the rich flavor will bring to mind all summers past.

Corn and Black Bean Salsa

1 cup cooked black beans
1 1/2 cups corn kernels
1 large, ripe tomato, seeded and coarsely chopped
1 green bell pepper, seeded and coarsely chopped
1 red bell pepper, seeded and coarsely chopped
1/2 cup finely chopped red onion
2 fresh jalapeño peppers, seeded and coarsely chopped
1/3 cup extra-virgin olive oil
1/3 cup lime juice
1/2 cup chopped fresh cilantro
1 teaspoon salt
1/2 teaspoon ground cumin
1/4 teaspoon cayenne pepper

Combine all the ingredients in a serving bowl. Mix well. Let stand at room temperature 1 hour before serving.

Makes about 4 cups

Grilled Corn Salsa

This spicy salsa is great on hot dogs and with grilled chicken. If you can't grill the corn on the cob, substitute 1 1/2 cups corn kernels.

3 ears fresh corn, husked
1 large, ripe tomato
2 fresh jalapeño peppers
1 garlic clove, finely chopped
1 1/2 tablespoons lime juice
1/2 teaspoon ground cumin
1/4 teaspoon salt
freshly ground black pepper to taste

Prepare a hot charcoal or gas grill. Grill the corn, turning often, until it is lightly browned all over, about 6 to 8 minutes. Grill the tomato, turning often, until it is softened and slightly charred on the outside, about 3 to 5 minutes. Grill the jalapeño peppers until they are charred on the outside, about 5 minutes.

When the corn is cool enough to handle, cut the kernels from the cob and put them in a bowl.

Peel and seed the tomato, chop it coarsely, and add it to the bowl. Peel and seed the jalapeños, chop finely, and add to the bowl. Add the garlic, lime juice, cumin, salt, and black pepper to taste. Toss well and serve at room temperature.

Makes about 2 cups

Corn and Hot Pepper Relish

Although this dish is basically a relish, it can be served as a side dish or salad.

4 jalapeño peppers, seeded and finely chopped
1 poblano chili, seeded and finely chopped
1 small red bell pepper, seeded and finely chopped
2½ cups corn kernels
1 scallion, finely chopped
1 teaspoon dried oregano
2 tablespoons vegetable oil
1 small onion, finely chopped
2 tablespoons white vinegar

In a mixing bowl, combine the jalapeño peppers, poblano chili, red bell pepper, corn kernels, scallion, and oregano. Mix well.

Heat the oil in a small skillet and add the onion. Cook, stirring often, until the onion is softened, about 5 minutes. Add the vinegar and bring it to a boil. Remove from the heat.

Add the onion and vinegar mixture to the pepper and corn mixture. Toss well and let stand at room temperature for 1 hour before serving.

Makes about 3 cups

Corn and Sweet Red Pepper Sauce

Dried basil will not do for this sauce. Serve it over grilled chicken or roasted lamb.

½ cup olive oil
8 large red bell peppers, seeded and diced
8 large garlic cloves, halved lengthwise
2 tablespoons balsamic vinegar
1 tablespoon sugar
⅛ teaspoon hot red pepper flakes
½ teaspoon salt
freshly ground black pepper to taste
2 cups corn kernels
3 tablespoons chopped oil-packed sun-dried tomatoes
½ cup coarsely chopped fresh basil leaves

Heat the oil in a 2-quart saucepan over moderate heat. Add the red peppers and garlic and cook, stirring often, until the peppers are softened, about 5 minutes.

Add the vinegar, sugar, hot red pepper flakes, salt, and black pepper to taste. Cook, stirring occasionally, until the peppers are quite soft, about 15 minutes more. Add the corn, sun-dried tomatoes, and basil. Reduce the heat to low and simmer, stirring occasionally, until the corn is thoroughly cooked, about 5 minutes longer. Remove the garlic cloves and serve hot.

Makes about 4 cups

CHILI CORN RELISH

2 jalapeño peppers, seeded
1 small red bell pepper, seeded and quartered
1 small yellow bell pepper, seeded and quartered
1 small onion, quartered
1 teaspoon ground cumin
½ cup cider vinegar
¼ cup sugar
1 teaspoon salt
2 cups corn kernels
½ cup finely chopped cilantro

In a food processor, combine the jalapeño peppers, red pepper, yellow pepper, and onion. Process until the vegetables form a very coarse puree.

Pour the pepper mixture into a 2-quart saucepan. Add the cumin, vinegar, sugar, salt, and corn. Cook over moderate heat, stirring occasionally, until the corn is thoroughly heated, about 4 to 5 minutes. Remove from the heat and let cool. Stir in the cilantro just before serving.

Makes about 3 cups

REFRIGERATOR CORN RELISH

To avoid giving this relish a metallic taste, use glass, ceramic, or plastic bowls.

3 cups corn kernels
1 small onion, finely chopped
1 green bell pepper, seeded and chopped
1 red bell pepper, seeded and chopped
1 celery stalk, finely chopped
¼ cup cider vinegar

2 tablespoons lemon juice
2 tablespoons sugar
½ teaspoon salt
dash cayenne pepper

In a glass, ceramic, or plastic bowl, combine the corn kernels, onion, green and red pepper, and celery. Toss well.

In a small glass, ceramic, or plastic bowl, combine the cider vinegar, lemon juice, sugar, salt, and cayenne pepper. Stir well to dissolve the sugar and salt.

Pour the liquid over the corn mixture and toss well. Cover the bowl and refrigerate for 24 hours, stirring occasionally, before serving.

Makes about 5 cups

Spicy Corn Chutney

This spicy concoction is excellent with chicken; it's also great on a cheese sandwich. It will keep in the refrigerator for up to 2 weeks.

2 cups corn kernels
2 large, ripe tomatoes, seeded and diced
2 large onions, coarsely chopped
1 cup currants or dark raisins
½ cup coarsely chopped fresh cilantro
3 or 4 jalapeño peppers, seeded and finely chopped
1 teaspoon ground cumin
1 12-ounce container frozen apple juice concentrate, thawed
1½ cups rice vinegar
2 tablespoons chopped fresh ginger
6 whole cloves

Combine all the ingredients in a heavy, 2-quart saucepan. Bring the mixture to a boil over high heat. Reduce the heat to low and simmer, stirring occasionally, until almost all the liquid has been absorbed, about 3 hours. Store in an airtight container in the refrigerator.

Makes about 4 cups

Iowa Corn Preserves

Don't let all the following information about home canning keep you from making this easy preserve. In fact, if you're new to home canning, this is a good recipe to start with.

When canning corn preserves, use only the freshest possible ingredients. Rinse them very well and remove any blemishes. Before beginning the canning process, read the jar manufacturer's instructions carefully. Use only canning jars that have been carefully sterilized; discard any chipped or cracked jars. To make sure the seal is airtight, use only lids that are perfect; discard any that are dented, bent, rusted, or otherwise defective. Preserves have a way of growing as they cook, so it's generally a good idea to sterilize more jars and lids than you think you will need. Pack the jars snugly, removing as much air as possible. Process the jars immediately and remove them from the processing bath promptly. Check the seals. The lid should stay down when pressed—if it doesn't, use the contents right away rather than preserving. When opening a jar of preserves, always check carefully for spoilage. If you can remove the lid without prying it up, the airtight seal has been lost. Discard the preserves without tasting them. If you note any discoloration, mold, cloudy liquid, bad odor, leaks, or any other suspicious signs at all, discard the preserves without tasting them. If the taste seems off in any way whatsoever, discard the preserves immediately. Refrigerate preserves after opening.

2 cups distilled white vinegar
1 cup sugar
1 tablespoon salt
1 teaspoon celery seed
1 teaspoon mustard seed
3 whole cloves
1/8 teaspoon cayenne pepper
4 cups fresh corn kernels
4 large, ripe tomatoes, seeded and coarsely chopped
2 large green bell peppers, seeded and coarsely chopped
1 large red bell pepper, seeded and coarsely chopped
1 large cucumber, peeled, seeded, and coarsely chopped
1 large onion, coarsely chopped

Combine the vinegar, sugar, salt, celery seed, mustard seed, cloves, and cayenne pepper in a large pot. Bring to a boil over high heat.

Add the corn kernels, tomatoes, green peppers, red pepper, cucumber, and onion. Cook, stirring constantly, until the mixture returns to a boil. Reduce the heat to low and simmer until the mixture is thick, about 1 hour.

Pour the mixture into hot, sterilized jars, leaving about ½ inch headroom. Seal tightly with sterilized lids according to manufacturer's directions. Process the jars in a boiling water bath with enough water to cover the jars to a depth of 2 inches. Boil for 15 to 20 minutes, counting the time from when the water returns to a rapid boil. Transfer the jars to a countertop to cool.

Makes about 5 pints

Spicy Sweet Corn Preserves

See the preceding recipe for Iowa Corn Preserves for information about home canning. For a really scorching version of this recipe, substitute 1 Scotch bonnet pepper for the jalapeños.

6 cups sugar
2 cups cider vinegar
3 cups fresh corn kernels
1 small red bell pepper, seeded and finely chopped
1 small green bell pepper, seeded and finely chopped
3 fresh jalapeño peppers, seeded and finely chopped
½ teaspoon cayenne pepper

Bring the sugar and vinegar to a boil in a large pot over high heat. Stir well to dissolve the sugar. Add the corn kernels, red pepper, green pepper, jalapeños, and cayenne pepper and cook for 5 minutes longer.

Pour the mixture into hot, sterilized jars, leaving about ½ inch headroom. Seal tightly with sterilized lids according to manufacturer's directions. Process the jars in a boiling water bath with enough water to cover the jars to a depth of 2 inches. Boil for 15 to 20 minutes, counting the time from when the water returns to a rapid boil. Transfer the jars to a countertop to cool.

Makes about 2 pints

Corn Preserves with Cranberries

See the recipe for Iowa Corn Preserves for more information about home canning.

3 cups cider vinegar
3 cups sugar
2 teaspoons salt
1 tablespoon mustard seed
1 teaspoon celery seed
6 whole cloves
1 2-inch cinnamon stick
4 cups fresh corn kernels
1 medium onion, finely chopped
1 small green bell pepper, seeded and finely chopped
1 small red bell pepper, seeded and finely chopped
2 celery stalks, finely chopped
1½ cups frozen cranberries, thawed and coarsely chopped

Combine the cider vinegar, sugar, salt, mustard seed, celery seed, cloves, and cinnamon stick in a large pot. Bring to a boil over high heat, stirring to dissolve the sugar. Add the corn kernels, onion, green pepper, red pepper, celery, and cranberries. Cook, stirring often, until the mixture returns to a boil. Reduce the heat to low, cover, and simmer until the mixture is thickened, about 20 minutes. Remove the cinnamon stick.

Pour the mixture into hot, sterilized jars, leaving about ½ inch headroom. Seal tightly with sterilized lids according to manufacturer's directions. Process the jars in a boiling water bath with enough water to cover the jars to a depth of 2 inches. Boil for 15 to 20 minutes, counting the time from when the water returns to a rapid boil. Transfer the jars to a countertop to cool.

Makes about 3 pints

Corn and Cabbage Preserves

See the recipe for Iowa Corn Preserves for more information about home canning.

4 cups cider vinegar
1½ cups brown sugar
4 tablespoons dry mustard
2 tablespoons salt
1 tablespoon celery seed
5 cups fresh corn kernels
1 large cabbage, finely shredded (about 5 cups)
2 large onions, finely chopped
1 large green bell pepper, seeded and coarsely chopped
1 large red bell pepper, seeded and coarsely chopped

Combine the cider vinegar, brown sugar, mustard, salt, and celery seed in a large pot. Bring to a boil over moderate heat, stirring to dissolve the brown sugar. Add the corn kernels, cabbage, onion, green pepper, and red pepper. Reduce the heat to low and simmer, stirring occasionally, until quite thick, about 45 to 55 minutes.

Pour the mixture into hot, sterilized jars, leaving about ½ inch headroom. Seal tightly with sterilized lids according to manufacturer's directions. Process the jars in a boiling water bath with enough water to cover the jars to a depth of 2 inches. Boil for 15 to 20 minutes, counting the time from when the water returns to a rapid boil. Transfer the jars to a countertop to cool.

Makes about 6 pints

Chow Chow

This traditional, piquant preserve was supposedly invented by the wives of the New England sea captains who prospered in the China trade of the nineteenth century and brought home a taste for spicy food. The time to make chow chow is when the garden and the farm stands are overflowing with vegetables of every description. Use this colorful recipe as the basis for your own version. See the recipe for Iowa Corn Preserves for more information about home canning.

4 cups cider vinegar
1½ cups brown sugar
1 tablespoon dry mustard
2 tablespoons salt
1 tablespoon celery seed
4 whole cloves
1 teaspoon ground ginger
1 2-inch cinnamon stick
¼ teaspoon cayenne pepper
2 cups fresh corn kernels
1 cup fresh green beans, cut into 1-inch pieces
1 small cauliflower, broken into florets
3 celery stalks, coarsely chopped
1 large green bell pepper, seeded and coarsely chopped
1 large red bell pepper, seeded and coarsely chopped
3 carrots, coarsely chopped
1 large onion, coarsely chopped
1 cup finely shredded cabbage
1 large cucumber, peeled, seeded, and diced

Combine the vinegar, brown sugar, mustard, salt, celery seed, cloves, ginger, cinnamon stick, and cayenne pepper in a large pot. Bring to a boil over high heat, stirring to dissolve the sugar. Add the vegetables, bring to a boil, and reduce the heat to low. Simmer until slightly thickened, about 10 minutes.

Pour the mixture into hot, sterilized jars, leaving about ½ inch headroom. Seal tightly with sterilized lids according to manufacturer's directions. Process the jars in a boiling water bath with enough water to cover the jars to a depth of 2 inches. Boil for 15 to 20 minutes, counting the time from when the water returns to a rapid boil. Transfer the jars to a countertop to cool.

Makes about 6 pints

Corncob Jelly

The flavor of this clear jelly is so delicate as to be elusive, but some people love it. See the recipe for Iowa Corn Preserves for more information about home canning.

12 fresh corncobs
4 cups water
4 cups sugar
3 ounces liquid fruit pectin

Break the corncobs into thirds. Put the pieces in a large pot and add the water. Bring to a boil over high heat. Reduce the heat to low, cover, and simmer until the water is reduced to 3 cups, about 12 to 15 minutes.

Remove the corncobs. Strain the liquid through cheesecloth into a heavy, 3-quart saucepan. (If there is less than 3 cups of liquid, add water to make up the difference.) Add the sugar and bring the liquid to a boil over high heat, stirring to dissolve the sugar. When the sugar is dissolved, add the pectin and cook for 1 minute longer.

Remove the saucepan from the heat. Skim off any corn bits on the surface. Pour the jelly into hot, sterilized half-pint jars, leaving about ½ inch headroom. Seal tightly with sterilized lids according to manufacturer's directions. Process the jars in a boiling water bath with enough water to cover the jars to a depth of 2 inches. Boil for 15 to 20 minutes, counting the time from when the water returns to a rapid boil. Transfer the jars to a countertop to cool.

Makes about 1½ pints

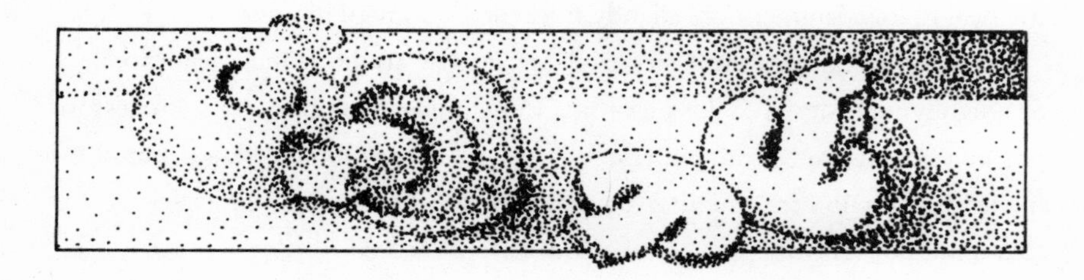

Corn Nuts

Large, late-harvest ears of corn are needed for this fiery recipe. A high starch content is important here, so use day-old corn.

1 teaspoon vegetable oil
2 garlic cloves, crushed
2 cups corn kernels
1/4 teaspoon cayenne pepper
1/2 teaspoon salt

Thinly coat a large, cast-iron skillet with the oil, using less than 1 teaspoon if possible.

Put the skillet over moderate heat until it is hot. Add the garlic and corn kernels and cook, tossing with a spatula, until the corn just begins to brown, about 1 to 2 minutes. Sprinkle with the cayenne pepper and salt and continue to cook, tossing constantly, until the corn is browned and dry, about 3 minutes longer. Serve warm.

Makes about 2 cups

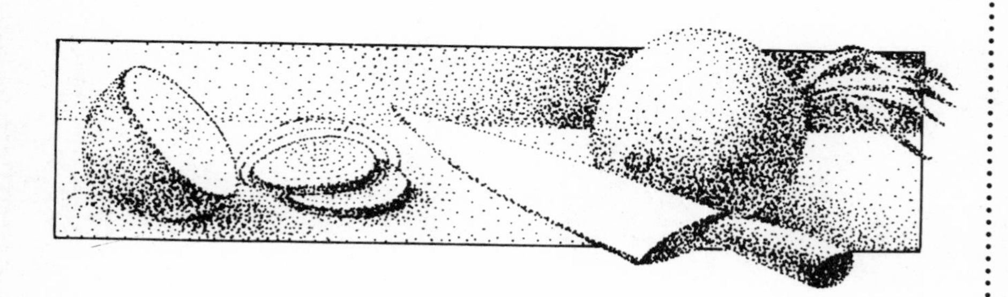

CHAPTER
13

Popcorn

Millennia ago, the earliest Native Americans harvested the seeds of a type of grass that was the ancestor of today's modern corn strains. The small, hard kernels grew on tiny cobs. To eat them, the harvesters placed them on a rock near a fire until they popped open. It's a far cry from microwaved popcorn, but the basic idea of a food that's easy to make and fun to eat remains.

Popcorn is a favorite American snack food. On average, a typical American eats about 56 quarts every year—a total of 900 million pounds of unpopped kernels. ✂ *Hot and buttered with a generous sprinkling of salt is still the favorite way to eat popcorn, but try the recipes below for a little variety.*

As a general rule, ½ cup of popcorn kernels expands to about 6 to 8 cups when popped. ✂ *One cup of plain popcorn has about 25 calories.*

BASIC POPCORN

You need a *large* pot or skillet with a lid to make popcorn this way. To make popcorn in a hot-air or other popper, follow the manufacturer's instructions.

2 tablespoons vegetable oil
½ cup popcorn kernels

Heat the oil in the bottom of a large pot or 14-inch skillet over high heat. Add 1 popcorn kernel and wait for it to pop. When it does, add the rest of the kernels, shaking the pot or skillet to form a single layer of kernels on the bottom. Cover the pot or skillet loosely with the lid and cook, shaking often, until the popping slows down. Pour the popcorn into a large bowl. Add any toppings immediately.

Makes 6 to 8 cups

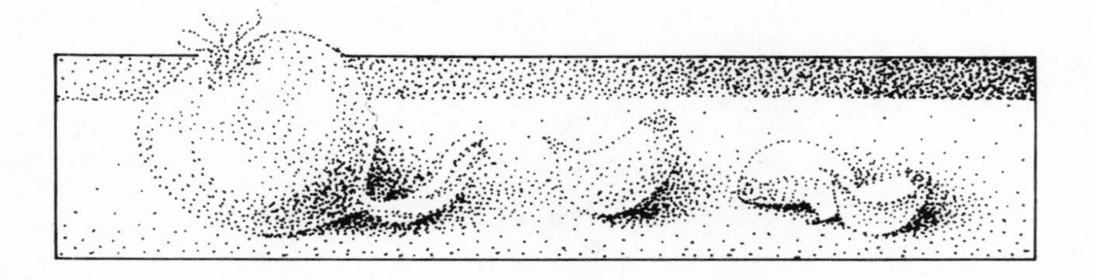

Popcorn with Cheese

4 tablespoons unsalted butter
½ cup shredded Cheddar cheese

Melt the butter in a small saucepan over low heat and pour it over the popcorn. Toss well to mix. Add the cheese and toss well again.

Coats 6 to 8 cups

Popcorn with Garlic Butter

4 tablespoons unsalted butter
2 garlic cloves, finely chopped
1 teaspoon salt

Melt the butter in a small saucepan over low heat. Add the garlic and cook 1 minute longer. Stir in the salt and pour over the popcorn. Toss well to mix.

Coats 6 to 8 cups

Tex-Mex Popcorn

4 tablespoons unsalted butter
1 teaspoon ground red chili powder
1 teaspoon salt
½ teaspoon ground cumin
¼ teaspoon ground coriander seed
⅛ teaspoon cayenne pepper

Melt the butter in a small saucepan over low heat. Add the chili powder, salt, cumin, coriander seed, and cayenne pepper. Stir well and cook 1 minute longer. Pour over the popcorn and toss well to mix.

Coats 6 to 8 cups

LEMON AND PARSLEY POPCORN

For an interesting variation on this idea, substitute fresh cilantro for the parsley and lime zest for the lemon zest.

4 tablespoons unsalted butter
2 teaspoons finely chopped fresh parsley
1 teaspoon salt
½ teaspoon grated lemon zest
freshly ground black pepper to taste

Melt the butter in a small saucepan over low heat. Add the parsley, salt, lemon zest, and lots of black pepper. Stir well and cook 1 minute longer. Pour over the popcorn and toss well to mix.

Coats 6 to 8 cups

PEANUT BUTTER POPCORN

2 tablespoons unsalted butter
2 tablespoons chunky peanut butter
1 cup dry-roasted peanuts
½ teaspoon salt

Combine the butter and peanut butter in a small saucepan and cook over low heat until melted. Stir well and cook 1 minute longer. Pour over the popcorn and toss well to mix. Add the peanuts and salt and toss well again.

Coats 6 to 8 cups

Maple Popcorn Balls

1 cup pure maple syrup
1½ teaspoons unsalted butter
8 cups popped corn
1 cup dry-roasted peanuts

Combine the maple syrup and butter in a saucepan. Cook over moderate-high heat, stirring constantly with a wooden spoon, until the mixture is very hot, measuring 250° on a candy thermometer (or until a few drops form a soft ball when dropped into cold water), about 3 to 4 minutes.

Place the popcorn in a large mixing bowl and pour the syrup over it. Stir well with a wooden spoon to coat thoroughly. Add the peanuts and toss well.

When the mixture is cool enough to handle, use your hands to shape it by cupfuls into balls. Cool the balls completely on lightly greased baking sheets. Store in an airtight container.

Makes 8 balls

Ginger Caramel Corn

6 tablespoons unsalted butter
⅔ cup sugar
⅓ cup dark corn syrup
½ teaspoon salt
1 teaspoon pure vanilla extract
¼ teaspoon baking soda
8 cups popped corn
1 cup coarsely chopped dry-roasted cashews
⅓ cup chopped crystallized ginger
⅓ cup golden raisins

Preheat the oven to 200°. Line a baking sheet with waxed paper.

Combine the butter, sugar, corn syrup, and salt in a saucepan. Cook over moderate-high heat, stirring constantly with a wooden spoon, until the mixture is very hot, measuring 300° on a candy thermometer (or until a few drops form a hard ball when dropped into cold water), about 5 minutes. Stir in the vanilla and baking soda.

Place the popcorn in a large mixing bowl and add the cashews, ginger, and raisins. Toss well. Pour the syrup over the popcorn mixture and stir well with a wooden spoon to coat thoroughly.

Spread the mixture on the baking sheet and bake for 1 hour. Let cool completely, then break up into chunks. Store in an airtight container.

Makes 8 cups

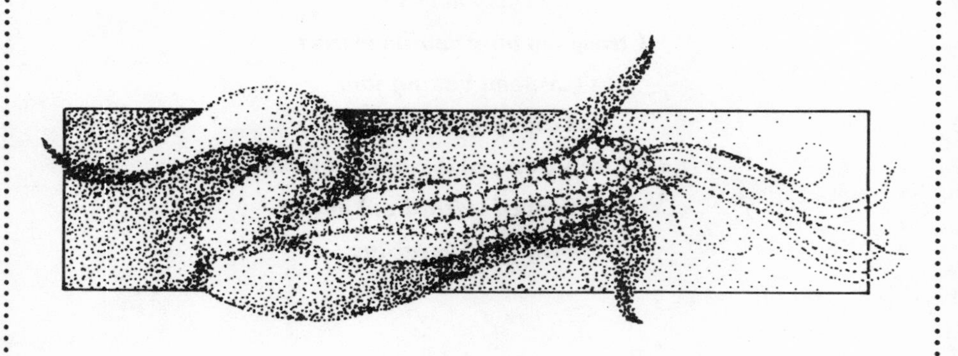

INDEX

Index